Where Did All

the Butterflies Go?

Where Did All
the Butterflies Go?

Elizabeth G.

WHERE DID ALL THE BUTTERFLIES GO?

iUniverse books may be ordered through booksellers or by contacting:

iUniverse
1663 Liberty Drive
Bloomington, IN 47403
www.iuniverse.com
1-800-Authors (1-800-288-4677)

ISBN: 978-1-5320-1169-6 (sc)
ISBN: 978-1-5320-1170-2 (e)

Library of Congress Control Number: 2016919408

Print information available on the last page.

iUniverse rev. date: 12/15/2016

DEDICATED TO
POPE JOHN PAUL II

When I was a young girl, my friends and I loved chasing butterflies. They were everywhere. We especially loved the monarchs. We'd catch them and then let them go. I don't see them flying around like they used to.

Did they all go away or did I?

CHAPTER 1

Before the Days of Me

My name is Elizabeth G. and I am about to put into words the story of my life. As a child, and even into adulthood, certain thoughts would fly through my head at certain events or even during conversations. My thoughts would say, *Elizabeth, you're going to put that in your book!* It was almost a voice; I now believe that voice was God. Now I intend to answer that voice to the best of my ability. This book is the truth and only the truth.

I have written about different occurrences in my life; some will be rather harsh, violent, sad, or miraculous, and somehow lucky since I am still alive! I'm playing down the romances. They all had a bad ending. Sometimes, when I recall all my memories, I find it hard to believe I lived through them all, as they were very painful and outrageous. The names have been changed to protect the innocent—me!

Many people have told me, and I agree, that I have an excellent memory. I can even recall my older siblings' relationships and their hardships. So I have put the various

1

episodes of my life together, and leave it to you to judge the unbelievable life I've lived.

My first recollection was living on Dorchester Avenue in Chicago's Hyde Park neighborhood. Although I was very young then, I do have many memories from that time. I was born to Arthur Sr. and Violet. My father was a union plumber, and my mother was a housewife. We lived on the third floor of a building that was not so nice, and I strongly remember there being mice. To this day I'm deathly afraid of them. There was a family below us with about seven kids, whom I played with as I got older.

Back in the 1950s, a union plumber should have lived a more prosperous life, but even as a toddler I knew we didn't because of our surroundings compared to other family members and people we went to see.

As I was growing up, I always questioned my mother about her and my father's childhood, but she was always reluctant to talk about it. I know my father was an Irish-Swedish Catholic and had two sisters. I couldn't find much out about his parents, except that they cooked a lot of Swedish food. I never met them because they already were deceased when I was born. I also know my great-grandparents migrated to America from Sweden.

My mother, Violet, was Hungarian and Lithuanian, and she was raised in the Jewish faith. Her parents migrated to the United States from Hungary and died when she was a young girl. She had many rich relatives; in fact, when she graduated from the eighth grade, her uncle flew her to New York to the Garment District where she could pick out all the clothes she wanted. However, her family disowned her when she married a Catholic, and she never practiced any religion again. In fact my mother became bitter about religion as a whole and didn't raise her children in any faith. I feel this hurt our family and created a lot of disharmony. Not everyone who prays or raises his or her family to pray has a perfect life, but I believe a little religion surely could have helped our family.

My mother said she was never sorry she lost the rest of her family (her parents died when she was young) by marrying my father because she loved him. So I wonder why there was so much bitterness in her if she married a Catholic. Why not become Catholic?

I know for a fact that she hated the Catholic religion, but it was part of her husband. I started to love God when I was only five years old, and I used to cry when I went to bed, afraid I'd never see him again. I begged him to let me see him someday. And now, I'm happy to say, I feel his spirit all through me.

My mother had a brother, Bob, whom she was not close to at all. From time to time, maybe every five to six years, he'd spend a few days with us when he got out of prison. My sister Teri and I were afraid of him. He always stole from where he worked, and to be honest, my mom didn't trust him and really didn't like him. But he would show up, and after about three days, my mom would say, "You have to go now." We never really knew him. We never even knew what happened to him except that he died, and it wasn't until I was older when I found that out.

There was a Chinese temple near the apartment and dancers performed outside. Oh, how I loved to watch them dance. I think that's why to this day I like anything Oriental. There are silly things I still think about, such as my mom talking on the phone and saying, "I'll give you a ring tomorrow." I always wondered where she got all those rings. There was a large storage company on the main boulevard near our apartment. I learned to write my name early on and the company's name was my name. I thought the company was mine, and the name was gigantic.

Later on, we moved from the Hyde Park apartment to a new one. We even carried a mouse in a box to our new place. Yuck!

Teri, who is three years younger than me, and I were supposedly "change of life" babies. My mother had us in her forties. I was on the shorter side, and my mother would always kid me about it. She said that when I was born, the maternity ward was run by little French nuns, and from them holding and feeding me I was little like them! There were record-breaking low temperatures in 1952, so when I went home from the hospital as a newborn, they had me so wrapped up it was hard to find my head. I was born into the baby boomer generation and have always been proud of it.

My younger sister was born in 1955. The sad part is not long after Teri was born, my father was diagnosed with lung cancer, and it was very progressive. My mother said he suffered so much that if she could have done it over again, she would have helped him die. This was in 1956. My memories of him were coughing and playing with me.

My parents hadn't saved any money; they always lived for the moment. But they never expected my father to die at such a young age. I did cry when he died, but I don't think I really understood it completely at the young age of four. Having no money, we had to move to a different area and into a housing project. There were beautiful yards and lots of kids and very little violence. There was also a big playground outside our door. We liked it immediately. My mother was quite an outgoing person, and she became acquainted with the neighbors right away. She had several friends that she would visit often. My mother wasn't your everyday housewife. Of course, she cooked us meals every day, but housekeeping wasn't her favorite activity.

CHAPTER 2

Not Your Ordinary Childhood

There were three children at home: my younger sister, Teri; my older brother, Arthur; and me. Keri, my older sister, and Thomas, my oldest brother, were married and out of the house. We all grew into our new surroundings very well. Arthur and I went to the public school about five blocks away. When I was in kindergarten, the monitors were eighth grade girls, who all wanted to watch me because of my brother Arthur. They had crushes on him. He loved that!

Even at a very young age I wanted the house clean. I remember trying to clean the house when I was four, and my mother laughed when I tried to mop the floors. But I needed the house clean, and I was going to get it that way. When we first moved into the projects, I didn't want to be ashamed of my new house. If I made new friends, I wanted them to think we were clean above all else. As I got older, I worked to make the house look pretty—not to shame my mom but she did learn from me and ended up loving a clean house.

My mother was on a pretty tight budget. She used to spend maybe ten dollars a day for food. At least that's what she said. She never discussed money with us kids. We could have one soda a day and we would make it last all day. I remember opening it and taking a sip and closing it and keeping most of it for dinner. Once I came in the house and there was a package of chocolate chip cookies on the table, so I opened them and took two cookies. At that moment, my mom came in and started screaming and hitting me so I hid under the kitchen table. She started hitting me with the ironing cord. I never could figure out why. Did she have a bad day? I think so, and she took it out on me.

We used to pass the Catholic church every day on our way to school, and I wanted to go there. I asked my mom if I could go to catechism and she said, "No, when you get older you can pick your religion." Although we grew up with no religion, I always knew about Jesus and God since I went to church with friends. Especially my close friend, Teresa; she was Catholic. She wrote down the Catholic prayers, and I taught myself the Our Father, Hail Mary, and so on. I was deathly afraid of dogs, and Teresa said, "Say a Hail Mary around a dog and it won't hurt you." To this day I do that when I'm afraid. There were several other things she taught me. I always envied her because she and her family did everything at the church.

My father had a sister in Ohio, and I would visit her on her pig farm. It was a lot of fun. She took me everywhere and bought me baskets of shrimp. She had immigrants working for her, and I sold the workers mud pies for five cents apiece. It's a beautiful memory.

My dad had another sister who was blind, and she was married to a blind person as well. They had two daughters. I loved spending time with them. My aunt was a well-established person; she and my uncle wrote books in Braille for the blind. She was a good cook and the one who introduced me to perfume. She had elegant perfumes in beautiful bottles. I loved to look at her collection. It was so different being with them; we'd take cabs to go shopping and eat at fancy restaurants. We also ordered food from the local pizzeria. I remember being sent to my aunt's house in a cab when I was little, but I wasn't afraid because I was eager to go. My aunt lived near Riverview, an amusement park, but we really never went there. They always had too many other exciting things to do.

The longer we lived in our new place, the more my mother got involved socially with the PTAs and community organizations. She was even the president of a mothers' club. Her influence got us into a lot of day camps and sleep-away camps and classes. Some I liked, some not at all, but Mom insisted that we go. Teri and I went to a seven-day camp in Michigan. On the first day of camp, my mom had to take Teri home to Illinois because she cried so much. I, on the other hand, stayed.

Before one trip to a very nice camp in Lake Geneva, Wisconsin, we were given a list of items we needed to bring. The night before I was leaving my mother had just come in from getting the items when I told her we forgot something. "We forgot the thongs for the beach!" She was so angry that she cussed at me and threw a fork, and it hit me in the middle of my head, making a deep cut. Blood was everywhere. She didn't take me to get stitches, but she bought some kind of powder and poured it on my head. It didn't work, and every time I moved my head too quickly, it bled.

When I got to camp, they checked for lice immediately, found the large cut, and wanted to know what happened. They were appalled when I told them. My mother was mad at me because they called her to tell her they were going to stitch my head.

On a different field trip one hot summer day, we went to a big picnic area that had an Olympic-size pool. Due to the one-hundred-degree weather, everyone was in the pool, including a lot of older, Polish-speaking people. I was in the deep water because I was an excellent swimmer; I got my junior lifeguard badge at ten years old. All of a sudden an elderly Polish man started gasping for air and going underwater every couple of seconds. He tried to say "Help!" and I rushed over to him. I pulled him to the side of the pool and tried to push him up and out, but the lifeguard came immediately. The man was okay, and he was breathing and yelling to his family that I had saved his life. His family wanted to mail me something, but the organization I was with wouldn't let me give out my address so the family got the organization's address. No one ever contacted me that I know of.

It seemed when I was young that the summers were always so hot. So one very hot July afternoon we were playing hide-and-seek in front of our house, and it was my turn to hide. I decided to go in the house and get a quick glass of water since I was dying of thirst. My mom was doing laundry, and to my surprise there was a tall glass of water on the sink. I grabbed it and gulped it down before realizing it had a bad taste. My mom saw me and screamed. I ran outside scared because I didn't know what I had done wrong. I stayed away until a neighbor boy came and said,

"Go home. Your mom's not mad at you; you drank bleach." So I went home, but we didn't go to the doctor or the hospital; instead she had me eat bread and drink milk. I had a very strange feeling in my throat, and it was always sore. For two years, pieces of rot that smelled horrible came up from my throat. God must have been with me. I have heard of people who took one drink of bleach and could never talk again.

I had to be about ten years old when I had surgery for a lazy eye. I was scared, but I hated where they put me in the hospital more. I was in a crib with all the babies. I was so ashamed. I cried and begged, but no one would change it. When I think about it now, I wish my mother had demanded they take me out of a crib and put me in a bed. Nighttime was the worst because they put a top on it, and I cried myself to sleep. Going to the bathroom was out of the question. They never came in because they had us locked up. When I think back, I hardly remember the surgery, only the crib. My mother did nothing about it and only came to see me twice in a week since she had Teri at home.

When I got home from the hospital, I had terrible itching and stress problems. I couldn't sleep well for about a year. Sometimes I wish I could still sue that hospital. Not long after that, Teri went in that same hospital to get her tonsils out. No crib for her and my mom was there to see her every day. Mom never realized how major my surgery had been.

I remember telling my mother that one of the youth center supervisors did not like me, but she liked my mom, so my mom didn't pay attention. Our group was having a Christmas pageant about the night baby Jesus was born. A woman was giving each child his or her part to play. All the girls were getting similar parts—a lot of angels—and then there was Mary and Elizabeth. I was the only girl given a man's role. I was very upset. I didn't want to play a man. I cried on the way home. As the days went by, however, I talked myself into doing it. But this woman never stopped hurting me. She'd embarrass me in front of all the kids and say, "Let me see your hands. Are they dirty?" They never were, but she still kept doing this. When I got a little older, she sent me on the bus to another youth center in a very bad area. I got shot three times with a BB gun, and the BB's are still in my leg. The supervisor said nothing; she just paid the hospital bill. My mother did nothing and said nothing.

My mother was usually home, but she did attend meetings for her various clubs now and then. On one particular evening, she had to attend a meeting in the evening, so my brother had to stay home to watch Teri and me. At this time, I was about six years old. He was eight years older than me and in his teens. My sister and I shared a bedroom, but we had twin beds. I was in my bed, and my brother came in the room and got into my bed, wanting me to touch his private parts. I kept pulling away. I didn't comprehend the whole thing. He became erect after forcing me to touch him; the rest was a blur. But everything is very clear now. I've never forgotten this incident or told anyone, not even my mother, until a domestic violence social worker talked to me and I told her. That's when the social worker explained to me that an event like incest could cause someone's decisions to become ambivalent, that it could have a lot to do with a person's actions in life. I believe that.

Maybe some of the roads I chose to go down would not have turned out like they did if I had gone another way.

When that same brother was just beginning to drive, he took me shopping with him. He had just gotten a car and wanted new seat covers. When we got to the store, he thought they were too expensive. So he took the price tag off of something cheaper and put it on both sets of seat covers. Then he said, "You bring them up to the cashier." Back then price tags would easily come off, so this was a pretty easy thing to do. He said, "They'll never suspect you being so little," but he was wrong. The cashier called for a price check, and when she got the actual price, I told her I did not have enough money. Then I went outside to meet Arthur, who was waiting for me. To my surprise he said, "We're going to do it again and pick a dumb-looking cashier." I argued that I didn't want to do that again, but he insisted. So there I went again. This time it worked, and that was how my brother taught me to steal. I told no one and felt very bad.

At a very young age I wanted a boyfriend, but I didn't believe that would ever happen. Ever since I was seven or eight years old, I had dreamed of romance. I loved the idea of falling in love, getting married, and having children. But my gosh, I never dreamed my romantic path would lead me to such a horrid predicament. I dreamed that Valentine's Day would always be full of flowers, candy, and perfume—surely not bruises, black eyes, and scratches. I guess the choices I made may seem stupid to some people, but I did suffer the consequences. So no comments from the peanut gallery. Of course, it wasn't what I asked for, but for a long time I was stuck in this predicament that wouldn't let me out.

When I was eleven years old, my friends and I would go to the movie theater to look for boys, not really for the movie. Sometimes we would sit with the boys, but when the movie ended, nothing ever came of it. We never kissed or even hugged them.

I was rather frumpy looking—short and kind of chubby with long, brown curly hair on the frizzy side. We didn't have the money for nice clothes so they came from discount stores. I didn't hold my head too high, but I didn't dwell on all that either. Actually some of my friends weren't too much better off than I was. At this time, I had a good role model in my eighth grade teacher. She was strict, but for some reason I was on the honor roll in this grade. When the teacher picked private students for field trips, I was invited. I was so proud of myself. It was the best I had done through all of elementary school. I even gave the class speech at graduation!

CHAPTER 3

Good-Bye, Childhood

I don't talk about my high school days too much since the memories aren't too grand to think or talk about. Boy, did things change when I went to high school! Everything was so much harder. I started at a high school that was about 80 percent black, but that didn't bother me. It was the only one in our district, and many of the neighborhood kids went there too. I liked going to school there; I had a friend who was black, and we had so many laughs. I remember her name to this day, but I won't mention it. That's also when I became friends with Loni. I knew her because she also lived in the housing projects, but we didn't become close till high school.

My brother Arthur was going out with a girl named Shellie, and they became engaged. Shellie dressed nicely and once gave me a big box of clothes. It was a transformation for me because I lost some weight too. I started wearing these clothes, and my homeroom teacher announced that we had a new girl in class—meaning me! I looked 100 percent better and felt wonderful too. I got a job at a dime store, and from then on I bought my own clothes.

Boys were really starting to notice me. Loni and I found a group of boys we sort of hung around with. I liked one in particular. His name was Angelo, and he was very good looking. He had dark hair and eyes and was a little on the short side, but I was short too. I seemed to go nuts over him. He started asking me to go for walks, and we would kiss. I was on cloud nine. He asked me to go steady, and I was ecstatic! Then he asked me to go to a White Sox game, but the problem was his friends didn't want anyone going steady. And I hate to say they won for a few weeks. About two days before the game, Angelo said he didn't want to go steady anymore. I was mortified. I was so sad that I felt like I wanted to die. I had gone everywhere to buy the right outfit and thought over and over how nice the night would be. My mom and older sister didn't seem to understand at all. As it turned out, we still took walks and talked a long time but never had sex. You could say he was the first love of my life—and one of the people who made me think, *I'm going to put him in my book.*

When I was about fifteen, I had a crush on an Italian guy. His name was Constantine; he even spoke broken English. I was working at a dime store, and every Saturday he came in with his whole family. I could hardly take my eyes off of him, but he never knew I existed. As fate would have it, one night my friend Loni and I were at the park we frequented. She got into a car with the guy she had been seeing, but I didn't leave. Constantine also was in the park. He started talking to me and asked if I wanted to take a ride in his new car. I said, "Okay." We drove around the neighborhood, and as it started to get dark, he decided to go where all the couples parked. We didn't make out; he only flashed his lights on everyone and thought it was funny. Of course, the couples didn't think it was funny. I felt like I was in a scene right out of *American Graffiti*!

When I was going on sixteen, my mom was planning to give me a sweet sixteen party. She rented a little hall in a building near our house. We were going to have pizza and cake. I was so happy because we usually didn't have birthday parties. My friends at the time were a little older than me, and I had a nickname, Tammy Baby; it was a popular doll at the time. Everyone asked me what I wanted for my gifts. Some of my friends had started shoplifting, so I guess that's why they told me I could've had anything. I told one person I wanted a fancy bra. The rest I don't remember.

Then the day of the party arrived. As my mom and I were bringing the record player to the hall, a few of the mothers came and said their kids couldn't attend the party because they were caught shoplifting! It turned out all but two friends couldn't come to my party. I was so distraught; there were only two kids and me at my party. It wasn't such a great sweet sixteen party, but we had a lot of pizza and cake left over, so that wasn't so bad.

I went to a few parties now and then, but not much happened in the boyfriend department. The eye surgery I'd had when I was younger wasn't completely successful, and when I got tired, the lazy eye would return. (As I got older though, it subsided.) I went to a party once, and it was getting late. This guy was there, and he either didn't like me or wanted to humiliate me. He started calling me cross-eyed in front of everyone. I thought I would die. Then he called me Clarence the Cross-Eyed Lion. I was so hurt that I left. I kept asking myself why he was hurting me. About two days later I heard he had been killed. I couldn't believe it. I certainly never wished it on him, but I wouldn't miss him.

Kiki, a good friend of mine from school, had a birthday party and some guys I didn't know were there—two brothers, Larry and Carl, and a Mexican guy named Jose. I found Carl attractive. He was well-built and average height, with blue eyes and a receding hairline. We started talking and were having a lot of fun, but then curfew came along. I called my mom to see if I could be late and she hung up on me; that meant no! So I left without making any future plans to see Carl.

One of Carl's friends got ahold of me and asked me to go to a dance club. I said yes because I knew Carl would be there and also because Blood, Sweat & Tears would be playing and I really liked that band. When Carl arrived, I asked him to dance. He said he was glad I did because since he was with his friend he couldn't ask me. This time, before the night was over, we made plans to go out for dinner. I was excited. He was about five years older than me and didn't do anything but work for his mother cleaning the house. I thought it was weird, but I was just going to date him so what did I care? My mother sure didn't think much of him, at least the part about not having a job. After all, I had been working since I was thirteen years old and through high school.

We went to a pretty famous Italian restaurant in downtown Chicago, and it was very nice. He even ordered wine. Carl ate bread with everything, including his salad. That's a habit I picked up. We walked around downtown a little bit and the night was pleasant. He didn't have a car, so we had to take a bus or double with a friend who had a car to go anywhere. Before I knew it, we became a couple. I did notice a big difference in his family with all the swearing—even at their own mother. Carl and his brother, Larry, had terrible tempers.

Carl's mother, Charla, got pregnant in her mid-40s by a man who was involved with some scary people and wasn't around much. Carl would yell at his mother because of her situation, but that didn't help her. My problems started setting in around this time. I never saw my friends anymore, and Carl seemed to boss me around a lot. One day we were walking down the street and he slapped me in the face. I didn't even know why. I was shocked; I couldn't believe it. I wanted to run. Then he blurted out the words "I love you." I stood dead in my tracks. I couldn't believe a man loved me, and I forgave him. But something funny happened when I got home. I thought I would be happy, but a dark cloud of depression came over me. I didn't understand why.

Needless to say the slaps started to turn into terrible beatings and mental abuse. Disagreements, jealousy, drunkenness, or just about anything else would provoke him. My high school studies suffered, and I started cutting classes. The school called my mother and had her come in. She refused to walk up the stairs so the principal had to meet her at the entrance of the school; it was so embarrassing. But I did stop cutting classes after that. Still I couldn't even think at school; I fell asleep in all my classes because Carl had stayed late the previous night. The depression was horrible. Everyone in my neighborhood knew that he beat me up, so any pride or dignity I'd had was gone. I can honestly say that my mind was so weak, I couldn't leave him. My mother knew he beat me and never said anything. Yes, he got a job and a pretty good one, and he also got a car. But none of it really mattered.

Carl had that receding hairline, and I had a deep front hairline. He always said my hairline was the sign of stupidity and his was the sign of intelligence. He hated my shape completely; he claimed I had a "pancake butt" and my breasts were not big enough. It always aggravated me because he would talk to me about other women's breasts, and I didn't appreciate that at all.

During my high school years, Martin Luther King Jr. was killed and all hell broke loose. The whole school was a riot zone—beating up white people was mainly what was going on. It was terrible. Loni's brother was beaten up badly. Fearing for my life, I made the decision to transfer to another school.

When I started high school, it was such a different atmosphere than my grammar school. There were a lot of Latinos, while in my grammar school there was only one in my eighth grade class. This didn't bother me; I was rather fascinated that they wore club sweaters representing the particular gang they were in. I had heard of gangs but never had been around them or seen girls who were in gangs. I never once, through freshman or sophomore year, said one word to any of the gang members. They were in cliques and only hung around with their own.

There was one girl named Sally who wasn't a gang member, but she was dating a gang member, and people sometimes mistook her for me. One day, when we were in gym class, there was an announcement that Sally had been killed. Her boyfriend had shot her in the head. I was so distraught about it. The song "Hey There Lonely Girl" was playing, and to this day it reminds me of Sally. I was never fascinated with gangs again.

I transferred to an accredited vocational high school, but I hated it right away. The school was all girls, and a lot of the girls were in gangs, so I kept to myself. I did have one friend I ate lunch with, but by this time my mind was already confused from my relationship with Carl. I really think if I ever went to my high school reunion, no one would know me. Yet the funniest thing happened in the yearbook. Under my picture was my nickname: Full of Joy. I had to laugh at that. One place I was never happy or joyful was in high school!

I did go to the prom with Carl. We were supposed to go with another couple, but the girl's new boyfriend changed his mind. So we went out to eat after the prom, and I actually was glad when the night ended. I had gained some weight and felt uncomfortable about how I looked. But I have to say Carl was a perfect gentleman that night.

One time I went to a barbecue with Carl and his friends, and his friend's girlfriend went to the bathroom with me and said, "You need to know Carl's cheating on you and he has been for a long time with a girl named Marla." I had heard rumors, but I didn't know for sure. When I told him what she said, he denied it. Of course, I believed it. On the way home from the barbecue, he was beating me so badly in the backseat of Jose's car that I tried to jump out. Jose pulled over and said, "Stop, Carl, or get out!" He stopped. And I was the one who just found out this bastard was cheating.

As I mentioned, it was all over the neighborhood where I lived that Carl beat me up. Everyone told my mother. They had seen him, but she never once mentioned it. A friend of mine was working at a restaurant near our house, and she was a good friend; we went to school together. She also was tough, and no one messed with her. One day Carl and I were walking by the restaurant and he started beating me up. She jumped over the counter and stopped him from hitting me. I never forgot her for that. Not even my sisters stuck up for me.

Another time Carl wanted my mom's permission to take me to meet the rest of his family in Michigan. My mom said it would be okay for me to go, so we took the bus there. When we got to Michigan, his uncle met us at the town bar. Carl was in the bathroom when his uncle walked in, but I recognized him right away. He had the same prominent, pointy nose Carl's father had. But I waited for Carl to introduce us. His family didn't go out much and didn't live too well. I didn't feel comfortable staying there because the house was rather run down, but Carl's aunt and uncle were very nice. I did my best to relax and fit in. We went other places while we were there, but Carl kept saying he wanted to live there one day. I knew in my heart nothing would make me want to live in that part of the country.

During the whole time we dated, we broke up several times because I kept telling him that I'd never move to Michigan. There finally came a time when it wasn't mentioned anymore. I know that Carl, who is now close to sixty years old, still owns property in Michigan and still has never moved there.

When I look back on another incident with Carl, it seems funny, but it sure wasn't at the time. We were dating and he didn't have a car. He wanted to visit his dad and his dad's girlfriend, but they lived in a high-crime area. I was scared to go but Carl wasn't, so we took the bus there. We got off the first bus to transfer to another one, and the bus stop was in front of a black liquor store. Everything seemed okay until two black guys came out and said to me, "Give me your purse!" Carl said, "Don't give them a f'n thing!" Then they wanted the ring I had on my finger. Carl again said, "Don't give them a f'n thing!" I was so scared that I was crying, and there was no bus in sight. The guys kept coming in and out of the liquor store and one of them said, "That's okay because the Black Stone Rangers are on their way!" I thought I would die. I was hysterical! Carl kept telling me, "Don't listen to these jagoffs!" Minutes went by and the bus finally came. We got on and left with everything we owned and weren't hurt. Carl looked at me and said, "Remind me to never call you if I'm in trouble!" It's still funny to me.

CHAPTER 4

A Wedding with No Bliss

Carl and I had been dating for over a year. It was Christmas, but not our first one, and he wanted me to come to his house while his mom was there with her boyfriend, Ernie, and their new daughter, Katy. Little did I know what I was in for. Carl was going to give me an engagement ring, and it was my own fault. We used to look at rings, and I'd say that I wanted to get married. I really didn't, and I never thought the day would come when he would buy me an engagement ring. But it came. What could I say? I took it and acted happy, but inside I was dying. I thought, *Why can't we stay the way we are, you by your mom's and me by my mom's?* But no guts, no glory, and now I was engaged. Besides, my family loved him in spite of him beating me.

The next course of action was planning the wedding, but I was in no hurry. During this time Carl took the police department test and passed, so he was on his way to becoming a policeman. This seemed to be the perfect time to become a Catholic. I wanted a Catholic wedding. I wanted to do everything as proper and normal as possible.

The priest insisted we attend the Pre-Cana conference. I was happy to attend the workshop, but it wasn't really helping. I couldn't even concentrate at a couple of the classes because Carl had beaten me up before them.

I went to buy a dress with my mom. I wasn't the type of bride who needed dozens of dresses. I wasn't big, so after a few try-ons I found one. It was very pretty, of course—white with lace trim, kind of A-line and low cut, and a long veil to match. Since my mom pitched in, I didn't pick a very expensive dress. She cried when I tried it on, but I always thought, why not when he beat me up?

The wedding preparations were going smoothly, but there was still a lot of stress between Carl and me. We got in a huge argument about three weeks before the wedding, and he beat me up. I had bruises everywhere and a black eye. His graduation from the police academy was that weekend. I made up my mind that I was not going to the graduation with a black eye and bruises on my face and arms. It was a hot, sunny day so Carl told me to wear sunglasses. "Hell no!" I said. "Everyone would know because it's inside; why would I be wearing sunglasses inside? And look at all these bruises!" He really believed I'd be there in the end, but I didn't go. He was mad. Charla said he was the only one there without his girlfriend. I didn't believe that at all. Even my mom and older sister felt bad for him, not me. I would not humiliate myself for him, and I didn't.

About a week after the graduation, I went to my mother and told her I wanted to call off the wedding. "I need your support; I don't want to marry Carl." Unexpectedly, she screamed at me, "You have to get married! All my friends are coming, and everything's paid for. You have no choice."

If only she'd been there for me, everything could have been different. But I didn't have that support I really needed. So of course there was a wedding, and I made up with Carl after that beating; I always did.

My mom and Carl's mom threw me a bridal shower right before the wedding. They held it at the hall in the projects. I was a little embarrassed at that, but my God, there had to be fifty people there. My maid of honor, Loni, didn't show up, and I was so hurt. But I got everything I could have needed to start my new life.

The day of the wedding was hectic. A friend of mine put my hair in an updo and it looked lovely. And when I put on the dress, I thought I looked pretty, but most brides do. I couldn't keep my mind off the fact that Carl had gone for a haircut. I hoped he got a good one and that it wouldn't make him look too old for our wedding day. If he had let his hair grow, it would have covered his receding hairline and bald spot. I asked him just to get a trim. But why please me?

My brother Tom picked me up because he was going to walk me down the aisle. It had to be 102 degrees. When we pulled up to the church, I saw Carl. He had the shorted haircut I'd ever seen him get. I hated it. I became depressed, not mad. He told me he even hated the haircut, and I didn't answer him. I was so disgusted. But I realized something later on: it wasn't his hair that bothered me so much; it was him.

Our wedding reception was a huge success. Carl had a big family, and my family came. We both had friends, and they all came. The Polish food was great. There weren't DJs at the time, so we had a good band; they played everything. I wasn't happy when Carl's mom opened the playpen for Katy on the dance floor, but I didn't want to argue and Katy was such a good baby.

We started to make our break from the reception around 11:30 p.m. We were going to a prominent Marriott hotel, and it was beautiful. Carl gave me sexy lingerie and a bottle of Norell perfume; I loved it. I was a virgin so the sex was painful, but he wasn't rough at all. It took a while for the pain to subside.

After our night there, we went out of state to a wonderful resort. The weather was hot so we swam a lot, and then we went to elaborate dinners; we stayed inside a lot too. The honeymoon wasn't too long because Carl couldn't take much time off from work, but I have to admit it was heavenly.

I sure wish I could say everything changed after we got married, but it only got worse. Carl thought he was still single so instead of working from 4:00 a.m. to 12:00 p.m., he joked and called it the "four to four" shift. At any time of the day or night, if he was home, his friends would beep the horns of their cars and off he'd go to drink with them. If we had evening plans on the weekend, they were always ruined because he would come home drunk and mean. And most of the time he hit me. Then he started this new savage thing: putting his gun to my temple and pressing it hard against my head. I never knew what he was capable of, but I didn't doubt at any moment that the gun would go off. Yes, I guess you could say he was capable of murder.

I joined a bowling team when Carl and I were newlyweds. He couldn't join because his hours at the police department interfered, so I went with his friends. He didn't seem to mind me going. I really liked it, and I liked that Carl wasn't there. I felt at ease with no one looking over my shoulder.

As the weeks passed, an attractive Italian guy started talking to me, and I could tell he really liked me. He knew I was married but didn't care. He started to talk about intimate things, but it wasn't dirty talk. He then asked me to go out with him, and I'm not going to lie, I really wanted to go. At this point I looked forward to bowling night.

I knew Carl's friends had seen me with him an awful lot, but they never said anything. And more importantly, they never said a word to Carl. I told the Italian guy that I would think about going out with him. He really kept on me for an answer. The bowling alley was in an area where all the Italian people lived. I can still see the image of him as if it was yesterday. I never forgot his name neither. I didn't go out with him because I hadn't been married long, and even though Carl was hurting me, I couldn't cheat on him at this point. Cheating wouldn't have made up for the abuse.

The Italian man eventually bought a bar in the area where I lived, and I went in his bar years later as a single person. He was married by then and was always going out with someone other than his wife. I had lost interest in him years ago. He would enter my life again when he started stalking me and got involved with some mafia-connected people who tried to terrorize me. He even threatened my landlord. I knew for certain it was him by the vanity plates on his car. He passed my house every day and night, and I lived on a side street. There were a good number of Italian people in my neighborhood with vanity plates, so I began to recognize people by those plates.

I had seen the guy with these vanity plates for years and then found out how much he was involved with the mafia. When my landlord tried to evict me for no reason, I got help and took him to court, but someone kept breaking my thermostat so I would not have heat. I won two months' rent to move plus the cost of getting the thermostat fixed twice. The landlord finally broke down and told me that the Italian bar owner had threatened him, saying he had better evict me. I told him I knew it all the time. He begged me to not say anything, and I told him I wouldn't. He apologized and gave me my check, and I gave him the keys to my apartment and moved.

It wasn't in me to get pregnant right away after I got married. So Carl wanted to travel, and we planned a trip to Las Vegas and Disneyland. The trip was pretty nice. Years later we also drove to Florida. That was a trip I won't forget. Going through Atlanta, Georgia, I had to climb in the backseat. Carl had started beating me while he was driving although I don't remember why. For my own protection, I went to the backseat and probably stayed there till we stopped at a hotel. It was a long trip. Our destination was Fort Lauderdale, and we got a motel right across the street from the ocean. We immediately unpacked and took our place by the pool with cocktails. As time passed, we moved to the bar. The motel bartender was your typical, good-looking, cool, and inquisitive bartender. Carl talked to him quite a lot. I was surprised he told the bartender that he was a cop; he usually wouldn't do that. Carl told him where we were from and I guess a little too much about us. Our room had two beds, but we made love in one and slept separately. We both went to bed naked. When I woke up in the morning, I blurted out loudly to Carl, "The door's open and I can't find my purse!" Without hesitation he stated, "Don't touch a thing; we've been robbed!" They took everything:

all our money, Carl's gun, his badge, and his wallet. They did leave my purse but took all the traveler's checks, close to $500. Carl said right away that the bartender set us up; it was an inside job. And it didn't help that we neglected to put the chain on the door.

We went to the police station to fill out the robbery report. Of course, we knew they wouldn't find who did this or get the stolen items back. But Carl needed that report for the police department, and we needed it to replace our traveler's checks. We did get our whole $500 because we didn't know the exact amount and had spent very little. Our trip ended pretty quickly after this incident, but I did find out something else that happened on that trip: we conceived a baby.

Early in our marriage, we had a couple over, and it was the first day I had worn my new contact lenses. I was supposed to take them off after eight hours. While they were over, Carl and his friend said they were going to take a ride so his girlfriend stayed with me. Hours went by and they hadn't returned; it was pretty ridiculous. So the girlfriend, who wasn't too talkative anyway, and I fell asleep. The men came home around five in the morning after leaving at eight o'clock the night before. Finally, the couple left.

The problem was I'd left the contact lenses in for almost twenty-three hours. When I took them out, I figured my eyes would be a little sore, but what I felt was the worst pain ever. I couldn't see and I was screaming. Carl rushed me to the emergency room at an eye clinic, and I found out I had bruised the corneas. I had to wear patches for over two weeks and live like a blind person. The doctor was pretty sure I would be okay but couldn't guarantee it. I never blamed Carl for that, but he did ruin that night. And I never forgot the horrible pain and what it was like to be blind. At least I thought it would end at some point, and it did.

We lived in a couple of apartments before we bought our own house. When we lived in this Italian area, our landlords were from Italy. They were very friendly and never thought twice about coming to the door with wine. But the funniest thing was they had a young son who always wanted to visit me, and Carl didn't like it. Their son had to be thirteen years old, and he could tell Carl didn't like it and didn't care. I always thought the boy was harmless, but a couple of years after our divorce, I met him as a grown man and he said he used to fantasize about me. He also told me that he still had a thing for me, but he was married and too young. Still it was kind of flattering.

Even though we never had anywhere near a normal marriage, I still tried to do things to make it pleasant. One night I decided to prepare an Italian dinner with wine and candlelight. I was working downtown, so I picked up all the food at the store. Carl's mother would be leaving soon for the witness protection program, and he wasn't happy at all about that. So I thought a special dinner would cheer him up. I had the sauce on for the spaghetti, and there was garlic bread and salad. Carl was napping while the food was cooking. Then the doorbell rang; it was Charla. She was all dressed up as usual with her jet-black hair twelve inches high. She said the food smelled good and asked if Carl was home. I woke up Carl and knew right away she needed something; it was a hundred dollars to get her hair done before she moved. He didn't hesitate and gave her the money. Then she left.

I couldn't help it. I blurted, "A hundred dollars for her hair? That's ridiculous." He wasn't too happy with my remark, but I thought that was crazy. Her hair looked perfect. Then he started yelling and said, "She said your spaghetti smells like crap!" He picked up the sauce and threw it across the room and then the spaghetti too! So much for our nice dinner. It never paid to give an opinion, especially against Carl or something he did.

Around this time, a friend of mine worked downtown at a fast-food restaurant. He called me on the phone on a couple of occasions to tell me that Carl was in the restaurant with a girl, kissing her with his arm around her. I told my friend I didn't care. I really didn't. He used to go to "watch parties" for work. At the end of a watch, the policemen would go on new shifts so of course they had a party! He'd come home with hickeys and say the waitress did it! The truth was that after the police parties, they went to the bars and God only knows whom he was with.

I'm not ashamed to say I stopped caring about Carl romantically. When I first dated him, I did care for him, but abuse took that away. I tried to find comfort in the relationship, but that wasn't working because of the abuse.

One night I was visiting my mom, and my younger sister, Teri, was there since she still lived at home. My sister walked in with her new boyfriend, Alphonse. He was a short, heavy guy. He seemed nice enough, but after a while I got the feeling he was full of it.

He said he owned a bar, which had been his parents', but then he said he was a policeman, not knowing I was married to one. I asked him which district he was in; I thought maybe he knew Carl. But he looked puzzled and asked, "What do you mean?" It turned out he was a security guard. From then on it was hard to believe him, too many lies. I would think to myself, *I hope he doesn't pass the trait to his kids.* My sister married him. He was very good to my mother, but I don't know about my sister.

CHAPTER 5

Baby Blessing

A few weeks after the trip to Florida I found out I was pregnant. I was happy about the baby. When I told Carl, he was happy too, but he said he hoped it was a boy. His mother let me know she hoped it was a boy too. This made me depressed because I kept thinking, *What if it's a girl?* I worked at a bank, and every lunch hour I went to church and prayed to have a boy or a healthy baby no matter what it was. But Carl was so obsessed with it being a boy that it ruined my pregnancy.

I was about seven months pregnant when Carl's mother was moving away since her boyfriend had joined the FBI's witness protection program. Ernie had snitched on the mafia so he had to move somewhere far away with his family. Charla decided to go with him. Carl was upset about his mother's lifestyle, but she had her mind made up. So Charla, Ernie, and Katy moved away.

Carl was still hitting me while I was pregnant, and I was worried about the baby. He sure wasn't worried though. And it wasn't long before Carl's mother, Charla, was coming back to town. She had left Ernie and wanted to stay with us. I wasn't too happy since I was eight and a half months pregnant, still working, and tired all the time.

When she returned, it was unbelievable. Charla was as dark as could be because all she had been doing was tanning in the town where they has settled. I had hoped she would look for an apartment right away for her and Katy, but she and Carl were too busy going out to bars. And when I came home from work, I was the babysitter. I was going crazy and getting disgusted.

One day as I was coming home from work, Charla was going out. She had left Katy with Carl. The problem was Carl planned to go out too and leave me with Katy. I decided to say something. "When are you going to look for a place?" I asked her. "We are having a lot of problems, and you're causing more problems. You need to give us our privacy. I'm very tired and ready to have the baby." Charla looked at me and then at my pregnant stomach and said, "I hope that baby dies inside you." I couldn't believe what I heard. She walked away and I went inside and told Carl what his mother had said to me. I told him I wanted her to find somewhere else to live. I didn't yell because Katy was there.

I ran a bubble bath, and he came into the bathroom, still getting ready to go out despite what just happened. I said, "Not tonight! Absolutely not tonight! Absolutely not after what she said to me. I don't want to babysit, just rest." We went back and forth, and he started choking me, threw me in the bathtub, and held me under water until I was unconscious. When I finally awoke outside the bathtub, he was hitting my face and crying. I guess he had trouble bringing me back. I was almost nine months pregnant. And he did go out that night. That night was the beginning of years of insomnia.

I never told anyone or went to the doctor, and I later found out I probably had lost oxygen to my brain. I was so beat up that I did go to a lawyer, and he took pictures of my neck where Carl choked me, my face, and even my bruised belly. I gave him a $250 retainer. The lawyer practically begged me to divorce Carl. He said he would serve the papers to him at work. I was feeling good about it. Carl came home after work and I said, "I'm divorcing you." He said, "Why?" I replied, "What a dumb question! They're going to serve you at work." He went ballistic. "I'll kill you! They'll never find you! You won't embarrass me like that!" Then he started hitting me over the bruises I already had. He was like a maniac. He also said he'd kill my child and my family. I was too afraid. I called off the divorce.

One weekend Carl, his father, and Carl's brother, Larry, went up to his father's trailer in the country. Now, I was at the point that if I heard from him, fine, and if I didn't, I didn't care. His father's second wife, Melina, on the other hand, was high-strung and very jealous. She kept calling me and asking if I had heard from Carl because she hadn't heard from my father-in-law. I said no but told her that it wasn't uncommon for me not to talk to Carl while he was away. Larry Sr. had just had a medical procedure done on his penis, so Melina was worried and called the local police. She told them, "Please do an emergency check because he just had surgery on his wienie and something could be wrong!" So the sheriff went to the trailer and told them what she said word for word. I guess the sheriff and the guys all laughed off the embarrassment. You could say that's really being desperate to get a call.

A few weeks after that I delivered a baby girl and named her Natalie. She was in perfect health despite all the hell I went through, and I adored her. Even though I did all that praying to God for a boy, I found out later in life how important Carl's daughters are to him.

The day I brought Natalie home from the hospital was a beautiful time, the happiest day I'd ever had. I couldn't wait to take care of her. I didn't even care that Carl didn't participate in her daily activities; I never expected him to. After a week at home, I got very ill. My thumbs swelled up and I got hives all over my body, even in my lungs. I was told the hives were from the shot to dry up the breast milk. I had to leave little Natalie because I was put in intensive care, but I went home as soon as I could. Carl's mother kept the baby because that's where he took her. I really wanted her back. They put me on steroids and I gained a lot of weight; it took months to get well. Stress aggravated the condition so I would have flare-ups when Carl and I fought.

Fighting was all we did. He drank all the time, called me filthy names, and denigrated everything about me. The less I saw of him the better. But one summer Saturday afternoon I thought we could do something together; however, he was gone when I got back from the store with the baby. I called the bar he went to because I saw his car there on the way home but was told he wasn't there. I waited and called again and was told he had left a long time ago. I decided to take a ride to the bar, and there was his car. I'd left the baby for a bit with my mother, so I walked in and there he was, dressed in an all-white outfit I'd never seen before. I walked up to him and said, "I guess you're not here." He said, "Let's go outside." Once we were outside, he demanded, "Get in the car and drive down the alley!" I did what he said. "Stop here!" he ordered and started slapping and hitting me wherever he could land his hand or fist. "How dare you embarrass me!" he kept repeating. Then he had me drive back to the bar and he got out. I went home and didn't see him for three days. I cried because of the terrible life I had.

I never asked him where he was, but a bill came in the mail from a resort where he had stayed with a female, and it showed all the purchased dinners, flowers, and the room. I wasn't even jealous.

Carl had a friend over, another policeman, and he told me to come out and warm up the food from the previous day. I wanted to go back to bed since I had work in the morning, but I warmed it up. I was afraid. I could hear the two drunks drooling over how good the food was. I finally fell asleep but woke up an hour later and put the rest of the food away. He had broken all the shelves off in the refrigerator! Why, I don't know. I went to work the next day all cut up with small bruises under my eye that got worse.

CHAPTER 6

Black and Blue

Carl and I could never do things as a family. The police were having an annual softball game and picnic, and he wanted Natalie and me to go. I was against it since there was going to be drinking; the hot sun along with the drinking really turned him into a monster. But he insisted we go even though I had to work that night. Well, we ended up going and thank God there were no scenes at the picnic, but when we got home he started all kinds of trouble. I told him I had to get ready for work, and he started hitting me, saying, "You're not going to work!"

I was in the bedroom trying to put makeup on my face because it was all red from being hit and upset. All of a sudden he locked the bedroom door so I couldn't get out. I didn't know what to do. Natalie was already in her bedroom sleeping. So I opened the window and jumped out. Even though I was on the first floor, it was a pretty high jump. I was walking with a limp at first. I didn't have the car keys, just my purse, so I took the bus to work. Several hours later Carl called and apologized. He didn't even know I'd left.

He had passed out on the couch, and when he went into the bedroom, I was gone. He offered to pick me up from work but I declined.

I don't think anything could ever compare with that cold, steel .38 Special he would press to my temple, and I never knew if it would go off. It was like Russian roulette, but I wasn't the one holding the gun.

One night he held the gun against my head a little too often and a little too long. I was deathly afraid because of the comments he was making like "I could kill you and no one would ever find the body." He was kicking me and punching me all over while I lay in a fetal position. Then he passed out. So I gathered up Natalie and her things and got in the car. I planned to sleep in the car all night, but it felt too dangerous. So I did something I dreaded: I went to my mother's house and told her how badly he had beaten me. She agreed to let me spend the night, but in the morning I had to leave. Oh, how I dreaded going back there. Of course when I went back, he acted as if nothing had happened.

In the meantime, Carl's mother found a new boyfriend about ten years older than her, but he was a wonderful guy, an electrician. He treated her like a princess. She didn't have to pay any rent or bills anymore. However, her ex-boyfriend came back to Chicago and called me, looking for her. I told him she wasn't staying with us. From what I heard, he shouldn't have come back—if you know what I mean.

I went back to work when Natalie was a little over a year old. It was a pretty good-paying job, but I cried the first two weeks because I missed her so much. I worked in the X-ray department of a hospital for about two and a half years and then asked for a transfer. But then my mother had a bad stroke so I needed to help with her care. The illness was a long struggle; no one else could be there so I was there as long as she needed me.

Every day was a challenge taking care of my mother and then going home and dealing with the mental and physical abuse. I began going to the St. Jude shrine for comfort, and it did help.

The holidays were hard because I had to handle them, and it was quite a burden. But being the perfect little housewife, I prepared a perfect Christmas dinner on Christmas Eve, and everyone enjoyed it. Carl usually was on good behavior around my family so everything went well, very well in fact. But New Year's Eve was another story. We were invited to a house party through a friend of Carl's. I really didn't want to go, but I had no choice. House parties meant heavy drinking, and that was taboo in my life with Carl. Not only that but he also would be off during the day so he would probably be drinking then too, making his behavior one hundred times worse. And that's what happened. He was out for a few hours, and when we were getting ready, he had me take Natalie to his mom's house so he could take a quick nap. When I came back, I woke him up and he started getting ready. I said that I would drive, but he said, "No, I'm fine!" But he was a really irritable driver.

When we got to the party, all they had was hard liquor and beer. I wasn't a drinker; I was drinking a Coke. He got mad and said, "This is fucking New Year's Eve. Have a drink!" I didn't, so maybe an hour later he brought a drink over and said, "Here, drink this." I said, "No, I'm waiting for the champagne." So he pushed me and started yelling at me in front of everyone, and most of these people I didn't even know. Right then and there I decided to leave. I acted as if I was going to the bathroom and I walked right outside. I didn't dare take the car, so I hopped on a bus. The party was on the north side of town and we lived on the south side, which meant it was a long ride home. All the way home I was petrified about what he was going to do for leaving him at the party. I tried to think of what to do and where to go, but I didn't want to involve anyone. Finally I got home. I decided he'd never look for me in Natalie's crib so I got inside it. I don't know how, but as scared as I was, I fell asleep. Around four in the morning I heard Carl come in swearing like anything and looking for me. He did come into Natalie's room and dragged me out of the crib, hurting my chest. He kept yelling that I had humiliated him. What a joke! I wanted so badly to spit in his face and laugh.

A couple of days later I was having trouble breathing, so I went to the doctor. He sent me for a chest X-ray and found that I had five broken ribs and a broken nose. And that's how I started the new year!

And yes, I still stayed with him. My feelings for him, however, were so negative that one day, tired of him constantly sticking a gun to my head, I followed him to the car when he was leaving for work. With his spare gun at my side, I had my mind made up to shoot him in the head. As he was pulling away, I called his name, and he rolled down the window. But I couldn't do it. I froze. I walked back in the house with the gun, so disappointed.

Carl was insistent that we buy a house. So we bought a two-flat building. It was nice but needed a lot of remodeling. I didn't particularly care for the area, but I didn't have the entire say-so on the situation. I hated when he had to do any remodeling because he was such a crab and screamed the whole time. Thank God for Charla's new boyfriend, Jim. He helped with everything and had a great attitude. It was such a nice feeling to have someone working on the house who didn't yell. In fact, he even said to me, "Why do you put up with the way Carl treats you?"

Carl and I went to the wedding of one of his good friends. I dreaded it because drinking made him so psychotic. Thankfully, he wasn't too bad at the wedding. I was dressed in a flattering, short, gold velour dress that I bought at a specialty store in a wealthy area. I hadn't had any kids yet, so I was really in shape and my hair and makeup looked superb.

After the wedding, all hell broke loose. We were having drinks with another couple at a bar. They wanted to get shrimp at an all –night restaurant. Right away this was a red flag for me. Since the place was open all night, most people there would be drunk. I knew something would happen with the guys being so inebriated. The guys went in for the shrimp, and the girlfriend and I waited in the car. I felt something was going to happen in there, and I told her so. Sure enough, we looked in the restaurant and a fight had broken out and the whole place was up for grabs. We cautiously went inside. The girl I was with went through a cooler, breaking the glass. She was bleeding horribly.

The police came as well as news reporters, who were interviewing everybody. Many of Carl's friends and girlfriends were there. One of the girls told me that a newsman asked, "Who is that lady? She's too attractive to be with her husband." I was a little flattered. The fight was with some Latinos. Carl and his friend thought the

Latinos were looking at them funny, so they were going to teach them a lesson. They all went to court; however, Carl received no punishment from the incident. I knew he was involved, but I never knew until the court hearing that he had thrown the first punch. I only knew I had a very strong intuition and knew that fight would happen. That girl who went through the glass had a lifetime scar on her face. It was such a shame.

CHAPTER 7

Baby Blessing 2

Then something unexpected happened: another pregnancy. But this was going to be a very different pregnancy. At this point Carl was constantly on his trips; therefore, I was alone all the time. I really didn't care. He went hunting on Thanksgiving and didn't call for five days. And as far as him wanting a boy, I could not have cared less. I prayed for a healthy baby. When I delivered my eleven-pound, thirteen-ounce daughter, his remark was "Another girl, huh?"

The day I gave birth to Chloe I felt like a single mother. She was the biggest baby in the nursery, and I was so proud of her. The second day Chloe was home I took her to the pediatrician, who said, "I told you to bring the baby in before she was six weeks old!" I said, "Doctor, she's only two days old!" The doctor and nurse were shocked by her size. We got a laugh out of that!

Carl didn't share my enthusiasm; not having a boy was a problem. He didn't even get us flowers. But I didn't let that take anything away from my bonding with Chloe. When I first took her home, I couldn't stop staring at her.

Who could care about her sex when she was so healthy and beautiful? Carl had plans to go hunting and said he couldn't change them because we had a baby. I thought it was disgusting! So the day after I brought her home, he left on another hunting or fishing trip, and I thought, *Who cares?* I was sick from all the stitches I had received, but he cared only about himself. What a piece of crap! I've always been glad Chloe didn't understand what happened when she was born. It was just her selfish father who thought he had to have a boy to be a man.

I started to hate him so much. I used to wish it were Carl whenever the news announced a policeman had been killed in the line of duty. I had friends working in his district who would call me and say he was out with girls, but I didn't even care. They could have him.

I went back to work after Chloe was born. I got a job as an ER receptionist, and it paid well but was the midnight shift. I found out that the midnight shift wasn't for me. It was difficult because I had no one to watch the kids if I slept. And Carl wasn't really doing much volunteering. Still I stuck it out; I was always tired though. The job exposed me to murder, gunshot victims, stabbings, and the worst possible homicides you could think of. I never thought I would see the things I saw in that ER in my lifetime. At first I was upset; then I became a little immune. But I have to say, I brought home a lot of sad cases in my thoughts. Working there left me with a very weary disposition.

When Chloe and Natalie were little, there was a guy in the area where we lived who happened to be a policeman, and he sold a lot of things. No one questioned where he got his stuff because the price was too good. Well, he was selling dollhouses—and not cheap ones—with real glass windows, electricity, running water, and all kinds of miniature pieces. Mistakenly, I bought one. The problem was it had to be put together. I thought Carl might enjoy this project since it was for the kids. God, was I wrong! We decided to surprise the girls, so he was going to work on it in the basement in a far-off room with plenty of light. The kids rarely went down there. You would have thought he was cursing at his worst enemy when he started working on it. It was ridiculous how much he screamed at the top of his lungs during this project. I heard every word upstairs and cringed at every cuss word. How could I have been so wrong? The kids even asked, "Who's Daddy yelling at?" I said, "No one you know."

Other people on our block bought the dollhouse, and they were doing well with it; some even had everything hooked up properly. So I thought maybe someone else could do it. Perhaps Carl wasn't inclined toward this particular thing. But he said, "No, I'll do it!" When it appeared that nothing had been done, I had to ask him, "Are you going to work on the dollhouse?" I wanted this to be over. Finally, after months of nonstop yelling, he finished assembling the house, and I told him to forget about the rest of the stuff just so the girls could finally play with it. Besides, they knew by now what the yelling was all about. He agreed. I can't say for sure why, but that dollhouse didn't go over big at all with the kids. Maybe because they knew how much he had yelled while putting it together. Maybe they would have been more enthusiastic if the electricity and running water were put in, but that would never happen.

Right before Halloween I got a call from my mom. She told me that she was feeling so sick. I rushed to her apartment and found that she had vomited everywhere and seemed lethargic. I called Teri and rushed my mom to the closest hospital. Before I knew it, she was in critical condition. I didn't realize at the time that I would never again know the mom I once had. Every minute she was going downhill, and the doctors had no idea what was wrong with her. They performed emergency exploratory surgery with no results. I was in a state of shock because I had not prepared myself for anything like this. They put her in intensive care, and it was touch and go. This went on for days, and I was at the hospital day and night. Then they put her on a respirator, which was really sad. By this time she wasn't coherent.

Because I was there so much and Carl was at work, my older sister, Keri, said she and her kids would help out with my kids. Carl gave her a hundred dollars to get groceries, and she bought ground beef and noodles; that's all. Carl was upset, but we didn't want to fight with the family. Her two girls babysat my kids, and Carl bought twenty-four pieces of chicken so we could eat when we came home. But they ate all the chicken. The same thing happened when Carl picked up White Castle hamburgers. We ended up having a friend of mine babysit the kids; our family cost too much!

It started to be months that my mom lay in this coma state with absolutely no improvement. She was being fed through a tube and moved periodically so she wouldn't get bed sores, but I did see a sore on her ear. It was dreadful. They played a radio because, they told us, your hearing is the last thing to go.

We had a DNR (Do not resuscitate) order, but she had a very strong heart. Only close family visited, but no kids since we didn't want them to see her like that. Her skin was starting to shed all over.

I have to admit I started to pray that God would take her so she didn't have to suffer anymore. Then one day I woke up and it was very cold outside. I was going to go to the hospital, but I got this inner feeling that today she was going to die. I had lost tons of weight and didn't have a winter coat, but I knew I would need one for the funeral. So I went to the mall and bought a long, dark purple coat and went to the hospital.

When I got there, the doctor told me my mother was in bad shape. He doubted if she would live through the day. I called the family as I'd done so many times before, and they all came to see her. I was staring at my mom and saw her change colors right in front of me. I ran and got the nurse, and she said, "Your mom has passed." And I knew my spirit was right; it was good. I called Carl and told him to break it to Natalie and talk to her awhile because I had to stay at the hospital to discuss the funeral arrangements. I found out when it was too late that all Carl did was tell Natalie my mom died and then he went to sleep. She said she was heartbroken. Chloe was too little to understand.

I thought losing my mom was bad enough, but what the funeral home told us was even more disheartening. My brother Tom had to hold me up from fainting. It seems the funeral director didn't think he could give us an open casket since her ear and part of her head had decomposed and even smelled. I was ill at the thought of this. Maybe that's why layers of skin had been coming off. He said it was an intense case, but if we bought a wig, he would try to have the casket open. So we bought the wig and were able to have it open.

But from that experience I learned that we're not meant to live on a machine. It was so sad and yet disgusting.

My sister Keri said there wouldn't be a funeral dinner because she couldn't pitch in, but I said, "Yes, there will if Carl and I have to pay for it ourselves!" I always think of my mom's wake every New Year's Eve because that was when it was held. But time does make you less sad.

My sister Teri and I took my mother's death the hardest. I think the other family members quickly went back to their own lives. I became ill after her death. I stopped eating; I just had no appetite. I had done a lot of things with my mother, such as shopping, going out to eat, and talking on the phone maybe five times a day. There was absolutely no one who could take her place. So I mourned a long time.

My mother had been long gone when the family made reservations at a resort, and Carl and I attended. My oldest sister was there with her family, and my oldest brother was there with his family. It was the worst trip of my life. I was shaky because I didn't like leaving the house anymore, but I did it so Natalie and Chloe could have fun, which they did. Everyone knew how Carl hurt me, and my younger sister had heard and seen a lot, but no one cared.

During the trip my older sister and my sister-in-law told me to pull myself together or I would lose Carl. Do you believe that? Well, I responded, "I want to leave him!" They said, "You're too ill." And I said, "He *makes* me ill with all the torment!" They looked at each other as if I wasn't there. After this trip I felt stronger because I wasn't really ill. I was living in fear, but there is hope. I felt it deep inside. Although my relatives didn't provide any comfort, their indifference made me angry enough to find strength.

After my mother died, depression took over me so I forced myself to get my hair done; I thought maybe this would cheer me up. I went to my friend's brother, who was a hairstylist. I'd always had naturally curly hair, but when it rained, it would get frizzy. He said I should cut it short and get a perm in order to have a pretty, natural curl.

I almost died when I saw the outcome; it turned out like an Afro. That wasn't what I wanted, but I knew I could live with it. Carl, however, would have a *fit*! On the way home from the salon, I bought glittery barrettes to put in my hair. When I walked in the house, he didn't hesitate and asked what the f— had I done. (He said the word.) He continued to ask me if I was trying to be black, and then he started screaming, "They want white hair, and you go and do this." He then proceeded to kick me out of the house. I felt ashamed because I thought my hair looked cute with the glittery barrettes, so I took a ride to see Carl's mother. She thought it was cute, but I knew why Carl was mad. I stayed there until the middle of the night and went home after he and the kids had gone to bed. I did everything I could to get rid of that perm, but as it loosened up, it was so pretty.

CHAPTER 8

An Affair Not to Remember

Not too long after my mom's death, Charla's boyfriend, Jim, came over one night while I was making pork chops. He had a friend with him about my age. Jim was seventy-four years old, and his friend, Tim, was in his thirties. Tim couldn't stop commenting on how good the food smelled and Carl offered him some, but he declined and kept staring at me. I guess I stared back a little too. I was flattered because he was cute, with blond hair and blue eyes!

I never would have thought of cheating on Carl until my mother died. My whole way of thinking changed. Now, the only person who really wanted me to stay with Carl was gone, and I felt stronger inside. Then the opportunity came but not right away.

The next time I saw Jim, he said Tim was interested in me. I was flattered but let it go. But things were so bad with Carl—the drinking, the hitting, the trips—that I decided if Jim brought up Tim's name again, I would mention that I was interested in him too. And he did mention Tim again. So I gave Jim our phone number and told him to tell Tim when to call. He called right away, and I met him at a bar on a weekend when Carl had taken the kids on a trip and I didn't want to go.

I met Tim at a bar outside of the area where we lived. I drank very little, and he taught me how to play video poker. We were laughing, talking, and affectionate. He was kind and considerate with no yelling or hitting; that's what I cared about most. We went to his place, and yes, we had sex, but I wasn't there for that. I just wanted affection. He couldn't stop commenting on how thin I was since I barely ate anymore. The night ended and I went home, and the next day Carl came home with the kids. I knew Tim wouldn't be anything substantial to me, but he was nice and gentle. It was only one date, but that's all it took. Guilt overtook me.

I don't know why but this huge guilt built up in me because I had cheated on Carl. I couldn't keep it in; it was uncontrollable. So after a few days had passed, I told him I cheated. At first I wouldn't say with whom, and he beat me severely. It was terrible; I walked on pins and needles. Then he demanded to know who it was. When I told him, he had a fit because he knew that Jim, now his mother's ex-boyfriend, was involved. He would hit me every time he thought about it, which was always. Then I told him I was going to confess to the priest. The priest knew me and knew that Carl hit me, but he took my confession and I cleaned all the pews in the church as my penance. I thought this would make Carl happy, but the beatings went on and on. I went again to the church, and the priest had me clean the church yard and the surrounding areas. Carl still wasn't happy.

Then I made dinner one afternoon and it was a nice one. He seemed okay while we were all eating, but all of a sudden he said, "I can't stop thinking of that son of a bitch having sex with you!" Carl started coming after me, and I ran into the bedroom. He pushed me on the bed and said, "I know what I'm going to do." He pulled my pants and underwear down and said, "I'm going to rip it out!" He began clawing at my vaginal area as harshly as he could. I immediately felt terrible sharp pains from his nails. This went on for a few minutes; he was like a madman tearing my vagina.

Although I was torn apart, I put my clothes back on. With no one to turn to, I went back to the priest and told him that I didn't feel guilty anymore. I said, "It's my husband; he won't forget it." I'll never forget his answer: "Why in the world did you tell him?"

I didn't think I could tolerate my situation any longer. I became another person in my psyche. I couldn't understand my horrible depression. Never did Carl say he was sorry. I never knew that trauma could cause a lifelong affliction both physically and mentally. I always felt as if something was going to come out of my vagina at any time, and I had bad flashbacks. There was no therapy for this, and I didn't realize why all this was happening at the time. But I do now!

I walked around so depressed, wishing I could die. I asked God to take me. I started calling suicide and depression hotlines, but they were no help. I had to go through the motions of life with a maniac and still care for my children. It was so hard; my depression made me physically ill, and Carl continued to be as cruel as could be. This may sound odd, but we went to see the movie *Scarface*, and I fell in love with it! I loved Al Pacino! So a couple of days later I wanted to see it again, and I asked my sister Teri to go with me. I didn't want Carl to have a fit or accuse me of anything. She said no but I still wanted to go, so I told him Teri was going. While I was at the show, Carl called my sister and asked her about the night. She not only told him she didn't go but also said she knew nothing about me going. She was trying to start trouble, and boy, did she! When I got home, he accused me of cheating again and beat me severely. Funny thing is the next day Carl's mom called and told him her friend saw me at the show by myself. But Carl didn't even apologize.

I evaluated what I could do and decided to see my regular doctor. I told him about my depression, and he told me to take antidepressants. He said they would take the bad thoughts away. He also said to give them a chance to work. I had a glimmer of hope. The doctor said the medication helped a lot of people and maybe they would help me. So I went home, took one pill, cleaned the house, and made dinner with some optimism. Then Carl came home. I smiled at him, and he said, "Why are you happy?" I said, "I have something to help my depression. The doctor gave me pills that won't make me feel as depressed as I have been. He told me to take one in the morning and one in the evening." Carl asked, "Why? How depressed are you?" I said, "I've been feeling like I want to die, but now I have hope." At the top of his lungs, he screamed, "No one needs pills. You're not taking pills like a psycho and walk around like a robot!" I said, "Yes I am. The doctor said they're not strong!" Carl said, "Where are the pills? I'm taking them!" He saw them on the counter and grabbed them. I was hysterical, so he grabbed me, shoved me, held my head down, and said, "You want these pills? You're going to take them!" Then he forced the bottle of pills down my throat. He kept repeating, "You feel like you want to die? Then die!" I immediately became unconscious. This happened about five o'clock in the afternoon, and I didn't wake up until the next day at noon. I was naked in bed, and my mind was all cloudy. I asked Natalie what happened, and she said, "You stopped breathing and Dad thought he killed you, but he would not call the hospital and he was crying." I was sick at the thought of it.

Shortly after Natalie told me this, my sister Teri came over, looked at me in bed, and said, "You're going to end up a bag woman. Carl said you kept him up all night acting goofy." I said nothing because she would never believe me. All I wanted to do was drive to my church and pray in the St. Jude shrine for hopeless cases or go to the church across the street and pray to the Virgin Mary for help.

Within a few minutes Carl walked into the bedroom and said, "I got to go somewhere; you have to take Natalie to softball practice." My God, I was dizzy and couldn't even think straight, but I attempted to take her to the park with Chloe too! Then I felt ready to pass out. I asked one of the other mothers to call an ambulance, and she did. The mother also contacted Carl. He acted so attentive, maybe afraid I'd tell them what had happened. My blood pressure was low and I hadn't eaten in a couple days, so they sent me home. That particular day Carl was nice to me. I wonder why!

Waking up every day feeling so low and unhappy was too much for one person to bear. Carl never thought any of the things he did or said to me contributed to my depression. He always said, "You need some balls." I used to think, *If*

55

I had some, I'd kick your ass. I had been in and out of the hospital, and every time the doctor told me to work on my relationship with Carl. I know now that was why I never got well. I did have brain trauma and many concussions from being hit and losing oxygen to the brain. I tried slitting my wrist; it was a cry for help.

I finally made up my mind that I was going to end it for good. I filled up the bathtub with water; got in it, clothes and all; and dropped a running, plugged-in blow dryer into the water. Nothing happened; it just vibrated. I guess God didn't want me yet. Natalie saw the whole thing, and I had to calm her down and promise I wouldn't do anything like that again. It was like a miracle.

After that incident I started seeing a psychiatrist I'd had from one of my hospital stays. But all he was worried about was the relationship between Carl and me. If you want to know the truth, I always thought the doctor had a crush on Carl. He couldn't stop staring and smiling at Carl; it was almost abnormal. He never agreed with anything I had to say. Then one day at the doctor's office, the doctor wanted me to be honest about what I really wanted or what would make me happy. Carl agreed, "Yeah, say what's on your mind; don't be afraid." So I said, "I think I want to start dating other people and eventually get a divorce." The doctor replied, "That's not the sort of plan that would work out." Carl was silent. When we went outside to the car, I knew all hell would break loose, and it did. He repeatedly slapped me in the face and head, screaming about how I had humiliated him. I took the beating and yelled, "You said to say the truth!" I was glad I said what I did. When I ended up in and out of mental hospitals, begging for a shock treatment, I knew I was losing myself! I was trying to make myself love someone, but I knew deep inside he was hurting me. I still have problems in my brain, mainly from trauma, but I don't frequent mental hospitals anymore. However, I will always need doctors and medications for past traumas and illnesses.

Carl was starting to worry about my attitude because I was saying and doing a lot of things I never had before. He knew things were different. He didn't treat me well throughout the marriage, and after a while, the bad definitely outweighed the good. The abuse alone was enough; there was no romance left. So I started talking about divorce and became braver. He knew I was serious. All of a sudden he was asking me why. He couldn't believe it! Well, I couldn't believe him. He didn't want a divorce at all.

Carl was making all kinds of promises to change and offers of gifts. He wanted to buy me a new Corvette, but I'd have to make the payments. He offered a full-length fox coat and a new house. The marriage could not be saved—at least in my eyes. Believe me, counseling was not an option. My mind was made up, but it sure wasn't going to happen overnight.

CHAPTER 9

Torment and Torture

I had a plan and wasn't going to tell anyone what it was, but a certain individual would have to help me unknowingly. The plan would go into effect the next time Carl beat me up. I called my brother Tom to take me to the mental hospital. When he arrived, Carl was about to hit me and Tom told him, "Don't touch her!" I really didn't want to go to the hospital, but that was the plan: to never come back after that. I asked Tom if I could stay with him for a while after I got out because I was not going back to Carl. Tom was glad and said yes, but he was hesitant because of his wife.

It's funny, but when I was in the hospital, nobody realized this was just a plan. So my sister Keri called me up and said, "Why did you sell your house to Carl for a dollar?" I said, "I didn't," and I hung up. See, her scheme was to upset me, but it didn't work. What a shame that a sister would do that!

When I did get out of the hospital, I went to Tom's house for one night, but his wife acted so weird that I called my friend Loni and asked if I could stay with her. She said yes. I was so grateful that I had a place to stay. I went to pick up the kids for the weekend and was surprised that Carl let me have them, but I had no intention of bringing them back. So the clothes they had with them were what they would start out with in our new life. Carl didn't make a big deal about bringing the kids back, so I was extremely happy. I wanted them with me always.

After moving in with Loni, I got a job right away. I would bring food home from the restaurant where I worked, and there was enough for everyone. I know this was a burden on Loni, having to drive me places, watch my kids, and listen to all the arguing among the kids. I had to start thinking about getting my own apartment. After all, Carl was calling and accusing Loni and me of being gay, whores, and other terrible things that were not true.

My brother Tom said he would lend me the money to get an apartment because there was a good chance he'd move in with me. Things were bad at home, he said. But within a couple of weeks, I went to his workplace and paid him back all the money he had lent me. He didn't seem too happy to see me. It seems he told his family he'd lent me money and they were mad at me. I replied, "Did you tell them you might move in?" He said, "No, and please don't tell them because I still might!" I said, "Now you can tell them I paid you back." He said, "Yeah, but I'll tell them I picked it up at your house." I agreed. When I left, I thought he was afraid to tell them I was at his workplace. How sad! So I was the horrible person.

It was terrible borrowing anything from Tom because his family was domineering and selfish. Usually I would pay him back double for anything I borrowed to please them.

I was doing pretty well; I had two jobs. One job was at Denny's and the other at a Mexican restaurant. I liked both jobs and made good money. One day Carl called Denny's. I wasn't taking calls from anyone but Loni, so Carl said he'd bomb the restaurant if he couldn't talk to me. (He never knew about the Mexican restaurant, so he didn't call there.) The manager at Denny's immediately called me into the office and said he had to let me go for safety reasons. The manager didn't call the police on Carl, just fired me. He said I made the restaurant unsafe. So I left and always thought that was wrong.

Besides losing my job, other problems arose. My attorney notified me that Carl was fighting me for custody. I felt sick when I heard this. The thought of losing my kids was a death sentence. I kept praying it wouldn't be true, but it sure was.

I got another job at a bowling alley—the owner, Rocco, insisted we call it a "bowling center." I would be the front cashier for renting shoes and lanes. Rocco was an older Italian man, with an Elvis-type hairstyle. He had a New York accent and wore gold chains. He repeatedly asked me to go out with him, but I always said no. One night I needed a ride home after work and called him. He came right away, and of course, we stopped and had a drink. We really laughed a lot, so I did go to dinner with him a few times. He was on the prejudiced side and hated that I worked at a Mexican restaurant. I continued to work there; it was my job.

Rocco hated Carl. Carl would call while I was working and threaten to kill me or beat me up. He couldn't believe a cop could get away with this. Rocco didn't care for cops;

he had been in prison. It must have been over a year or so after I left the bowling alley that I heard from Rocco. He called and asked if I'd go to New York with him. I told him I'd let him know but never did. He had told me things that he might have regretted, and I was afraid that would be a one-way trip!

It was kind of funny that even though I had moved out of Loni's, she still got phone calls for me. I had acquired a social life, and dating wasn't hard for me at this time. I asked Loni to give me a ride to get a haircut one afternoon, and she agreed to do so. We were on our way, and I was talking about work. Right in the middle of the conversation, she said, "I don't know why you've met so many people and they still call. You're not even pretty." Not expecting this, I just said, "I know." Then she added, "You may be attractive to men, but you're not pretty." I was silent; what else could I say? I do know that all Loni's life her family told her how beautiful she was. I thought she was pretty. But why humiliate me? I already thought I wasn't pretty. I never forgot her words.

I started to commute back and forth from the suburbs to court. Carl and I had to see a psychiatrist and a mediator to determine who would get the kids, but the final judgment would come from the judge. After a few sessions, the mediator was leaning toward Carl because his mother was going to help him raise them, which was a lie. I was owed thousands of dollars in back child support too!

The state's attorney assured me I'd get all that back child support. For over a year I didn't receive hardly anything. And I had proof. In the final court hearing, the judge gave me custody of my children, thank God, and my house in Chicago.

But in the child support hearing, in another court, the judge walked in and started talking to Carl's attorney about the golf game they had played the day before. I knew right then and there I would lose the case. I received no back support and no child support through the court, not even an insurance card for my kids. My lawyer was laughing and talking to Carl's lawyer as if he worked for him. When I asked why I lost, the lawyer said there was a loophole. I said more like a golf hole! I wanted to turn the whole bunch of them in to the bar association. A couple of months later, the Greylord scandal surfaced, and I heard this judge was involved. I have no trust in the judicial system. Even the state's attorneys shook their heads.

During the time I was running back and forth to court, my oldest sister, Keri, had open-heart surgery and wasn't doing well. She wasn't too happy that I was divorcing Carl. Actually I thought she was envious because her life was so bad with her husband, but she didn't have the nerve to leave him. And she was always complaining about her kids too.

When I went to visit her, she talked about her husband's cheating and that she knew she was going to die. I told her she was not going to die. The doctor had said she had an infection, and her depression wouldn't let her fight it. One night I worked late and when I got home, my friend Loni called and said my sister had died. I was shocked. Loni drove me to Chicago, and we went right to the hospital. I walked in as the black sheep. Nobody talked to me, so I went to see her body and then Loni and I left. No one spoke one word to me.

On the way to my sister's wake, a car kept hitting my bumper; it was Carl. I pulled over, and he said, "I'm going to the wake too!" When I got there, again no one would speak to me. My kids were with me and didn't leave my side. We heard my nieces say, "Why did she bring the kids?" Maybe because Keri was their aunt, that's why! Everyone was laughing and talking to Carl, except my brother Tom. He stayed to himself. My oldest niece's husband approached me and said, "Don't you feel guilty?" and I thought to myself, *Hell no*!

The funeral was no different and I hardly stayed for the dinner. What a family. I asked my brother-in-law if we could stay in touch, and he came right out and said no! Well, I didn't know he sued the hospital and got a big settlement. Then he married the woman he had been cheating with. But sometimes things don't work out. I understand that after marrying the woman, she lost her legs. What a tragedy. But would Keri think so? I doubt that.

Even though I was living in Chicago, I decided to commute five days a week to the Mexican restaurant in the suburbs since the money was pretty good. On the first day I drove from Chicago to the restaurant, I worked the lunch shift. For the first half hour the place was empty. Then about six men in business suits came in and I kidded with them, asking if they had reservations. They were extremely serious and flashed their badges. They were from the FBI and had come to close down the restaurant. They went right to the owner, cook, and busboys and handcuffed them, everyone but me. Then they asked me if I was owed any money. I was so nervous I said no even though they did owe me money. They told me I was free to go, that I didn't do anything wrong. All the way home I kept looking for a police car to come or follow me, but nothing happened. The next day Loni called and told me that the restaurant was a front and had been busted for its connection to a famous Mexican cartel. Out of fear, I will not give the name.

CHAPTER 10

Rebirth

So I lost my restaurant job and what a shocking way to lose it. On top of that, when I returned to the Chicago house, where Carl had been living all the time I was gone, he hadn't paid the gas bill and it was up to $1,000. He expected me to pay it. I said I had no intention of paying it; I had my own bills to pay. My brother Tom, who was an executive at the gas company, told me to show proof that I lived elsewhere and paid the bills there. He also helped me to get a lien on Carl's check to pay the gas bill. Carl hated Tom for that.

Rarely did my family help me, but this time Tom did. Still I had no real family to turn to when I came back, so I made friends with the girl across the street, Mickey. She was always there for me as I was for her. She was a little younger than me but not by much. Mickey not only was a friend but she also helped out with the kids and they liked her.

Trying to straighten out my life was a big ordeal. I was diagnosed with PTSD (post-traumatic stress disorder) like the soldiers who were at war. I had a difficult time holding a job for any length of time. My psychiatrist recommended

I go on Social Security disability and I got it. It helped a lot financially because my child support was not coming through. The court had never specified an amount as it was supposed to do so Carl and I agreed upon an amount. Since Carl was always crying broke he barely paid me child support.

I haven't mentioned much about Carl's father, Larry Sr., or his brother maybe because I'm just not happy talking about things I don't have to! Carl's parents were divorced when Carl was young. His father was an alcoholic and also violent from what I was told. Carl still kept in touch with him, and he had a wife from southern Tennessee. I believe she was only concerned about her children and could not have cared less about Carl and his brother. His father, not seeming to have a mind of his own, did nothing for his sons either.

We gave Carl's dad beautiful grandchildren, and we would go to their house for the holidays with gifts for them. They didn't give us anything, not even presents for the kids. Larry Sr. would go in the freezer and pull out a stack of money he received as a commission for the year, and it was thousands of dollars. But not a dollar for his grandchildren. Even when we went out to eat, Carl had to pick up the bill.

But that wasn't my main reason for disliking them. They disrespected me during the hardest time of my life. When my mother died, they didn't call or come to the funeral, and when it was all over, they came to visit. I told them both what I thought of them.

Carl's brother, Larry, was a pain in my you-know-what. For some reason Carl had this need to cater to Larry, and it was ridiculous. We bought a property with him and his wife, and I don't think they ever contributed any money for it. I doubt there was any profit in this investment; it was a big screw-over.

The worst was the time Carl put Larry's name on a football square and they won. Larry never paid Carl a cent to place that bet. But when Carl's square came in—and it was a lot of money—he told me, "I have to give my brother half." I asked, "Did he pay for the square yet?" Carl replied, "No, he didn't," but said he was giving him half anyway. The most irritating thing was when Carl dropped off the winnings, Larry actually counted the money in front of us to make sure it was all there! Carl was really mad, but he still didn't learn not to cater to Larry.

One nice thing Carl's brother did do was on the morning of my mother's funeral, he came over with a dozen donuts and coffee for us. I found that very kind.

After returning to my house, I hadn't quite unpacked everything, and as I was going through some pictures, one stood out. It was a picture of me at my wedding to Carl in front of the Blessed Virgin Mary. All over the picture were red teardrops. I was amazed and could think of no explanation for these teardrops.

So I wrote a letter to the Pope at the Vatican and asked him, "If this is a sacred picture, will you keep it for me?" He thanked me but did not send back the picture. I know in my heart that all the times I went crying to Mary she had heard me.

After getting back to my house, I figured it was time to start my new life. Right away I got a waitress job but very little child support. There was a bar around the corner from my house so now and then I would go there. I was still friendly with the girl across the street, Mickey. At this point Loni and I had grown apart, which was mostly her doing.

I had quite a few tenants for the second-floor apartment in the apartment building I owned and lived in after the divorce. Carl referred a policeman named Joe to me to rent the apartment, and being a single policeman, I didn't see a problem. So everything was working out. Carl often asked about him, and I'd say, "He's fine." I played music a lot instead of the TV, and this bugged Carl. When he came for the kids, he'd always say, "Why is that shit on?" and I would say, "You mean music?" One time he came for the kids and said, "Joe can't stand your loud music; it's like living above a bar!" I replied, "What a lie!" I told Carl I was going to talk to Joe, and then he shut up. I did talk to Joe, who told me he never said that. Carl had asked him, "How can you stand all the noise?" and he answered, "What noise?" Carl just wanted to control every aspect of my life and wanted the music to stop.

You would think that most men would like their woman to have long hair but not Carl. The shorter the better for him. So for almost fifteen years I had short hair, except when I let it grow a little longer to look like Princess Diana. It was cute. After the divorce, for the next couple of years, I let my hair grow long and wore it on the wild side. Men really liked it. Most of all I liked it too!

When Carl picked up the kids for his weekends with them, he felt it was his business to go through my private things like my mail, drawers, and closets. A few times he put the kids in the car and said he'd be right back. Then he came back in the house and tried to fool around with me, but I wasn't going to have it. I had to laugh the last time this happened. He asked me why I never grew my hair like that for him. I thought to myself, *He wouldn't let me.*

Most of my employment after the divorce consisted of waitressing in Greek restaurants and bartending. The only problem was that the Greeks were very hard on their help. If they disrespected me too much, I always walked out. Both waitressing and bartending brought in a pretty good salary, but you could never count on it on a daily basis.

While working as a bartender at a nice hotel, I also had to cook food on certain days. It was next to impossible to keep up because two people were required for this job, one to cook and one to bartend. The place got crowded on the nights when there was a band, so I was super busy and working my butt off. One night I heard a huge food order come over the intercom from my boss. The boss was a girl who was my age, and she was dating the owner of the hotel. I was going as fast as I could. There were fifty seats at the bar, and they were all full. So were the tables. Maybe ten minutes went by, but there were still around four minutes left until the big order was ready. The intercom came on and the boss said, "Where the F is my food, you slow bitch?" Everyone started laughing.

I didn't find this funny, and I removed my apron and walked away. As I was walking, one of the maintenance guys came up to me and said, "Don't leave this upset; let's talk. I have an office downstairs." Not thinking, I went. But when we went into the office, he locked us in. I was in immediate danger. At least I thought so. I asked him why he locked the door, and he said, "For privacy, in case they look for me." I said I would feel better with the door open, but he said, "When you were leaving, you seemed upset, and I wouldn't want you to drive like that." He was very good looking, but I didn't care; I was afraid. He went on to tell me that my boss treated everyone like that, meaning the bartenders. Basically, he was telling me not to take it personally. He was talking a lot, but I was afraid he'd kill me and no one would find me. I kept repeating, "Help me, God!" over and over again. It got to be ten o'clock and I lied to him, saying, "You've helped me a lot, but I was off at ten o'clock and have to pick up my kids." To my surprise, he unlocked the door, walked me to my car, and told me to be careful. I thanked God right then and there.

The kids seemed to be happy enough. I was glad because they had done a lot of moving. One night I met a much older man named Allen. He asked me for a date and I said yes. I wasn't at all romantically interested in him though. I didn't intend to see Rocco again, and I even went to confession for dating him. On the first date, Allen took me to a bar featuring female impersonators. I didn't know at the time but his wife had left him because she was gay. He wanted to see if I had gay tendencies, and I guess I passed the test. Allen was like a sugar daddy until another guy came into my life named Nick.

Nick was an Italian guy I met in the bar near my house, and we constantly flirted with each other. One night, in front of Allen, he asked me to go to a party with him and I said I wished I could. Nick would sit down next to Allen and me and hold my hand. I liked Nick so much I didn't care. Then one night I went to the bar with a friend and he was in there. We ended up taking a ride. It was so romantic; we had champagne and made out. He said to me, "Don't tell anyone," but the next day he told all his friends. He didn't have a girlfriend, but I had Allen.

CHAPTER 11

Up in Smoke

One day when my friend Mickey and I were sitting in my living room, Chloe ran up from the basement screaming there was a fire downstairs. Mickey and I ran downstairs, but it was out of control and we had to call 911. Although we attempted to put out the fire, it was spreading through the floor. No one got hurt, but we couldn't live there because there was too much damage. I had good homeowner's insurance, so I could have the house completely rehabbed. My kids and I stayed across the street at Mickey's house, and we got new furniture and replaced all the items in our house. It turned out to be a blessing in disguise.

Carl heard about the fire and came rushing over to find out how it started. Chloe and her friend had been playing with candles that keep lighting when you blow them out. So he went to yell at Chloe. The fireman told him not to yell at her; she felt guilty enough. The house was pretty open, and a lot of stuff disappeared, such as jewelry and other valuables. Some said it was the firemen, but I disagreed and thought it was the gang members in the area. One day my sister Teri stopped by Mickey's house, and we just had come back from shopping for new clothes with some of the leftover money from the insurance settlement. It upset her so badly that she had to leave. She even stopped talking to me although I had just thrown her a baby shower. I could never win with my family.

No one in my family offered to lend a hand. In fact, on the day of the fire, the whole neighborhood was out there, and my sister Teri came and left while I was talking to the firemen. She gave $2.47 to a friend of ours to give me and said she'd call me the next day. I laughed and said, "Where?" Where would she call me since my house was condemned? That was my family for you. I asked my oldest brother to help me hire a company to repair the house, but he said he didn't have time. I had tons of ambulance chasers, lawyers, and rehab companies hounding me, but everything came out okay. I did a great job.

Even though I was divorced from Carl, I had to call the police a lot on him. And let me tell you, in the eighties a policeman could break the law over and over and get away with it.

I had a bad habit of leaving the front door open, but the only bad guy who would sneak in was Carl. He'd hide in the living room and listen to my phone calls if I was on the phone in the kitchen. He also would walk in the bathroom while I was in the bathtub and scare me to death.

I started locking the door, and he actually broke the door in and the whole framework. When I called the police on him, he told them I was a psychiatric patient. Finally I told his new wife, and things changed after that. But the last time he showed up, the police were so fed up with him that they came with their guns drawn. Carl ran out the back door.

I went out one evening for dinner with Allen, and we went to a Mexican place we liked. During the night I didn't feel well, so I awoke several times and went to the bathroom in the dark and kept vomiting. I didn't notice what I vomited. The last time I went to the bathroom I fell and noticed blood all over the floor.

My daughter Natalie woke up and must have heard me, and she called her father. He called an ambulance. I was in and out of consciousness, and as the EMTs took me out, they said, "She's going into shock; she's lost too much blood!" All the vomiting had been blood. Carl told the kids I got sick from drinking too much, but I hadn't been drinking in a while. I was angry. I was put into intensive care and given a blood transfusion, but I was still in bad shape. The priest prayed over me, which really scared me. I had to stay in the hospital a good two weeks and started to get well.

When I got out of the hospital, Allen wasn't too nice to me despite all I'd been through. My next step was to break up with him, and in the next few months I did just that.

I was supposed to follow up with a surgeon because I'd had a bleeding ulcer, but I never did. Thank God I was okay even though I never went for a checkup. One Saturday night I was watching TV at home and got a call around nine o'clock. It was Nick. He sounded upset and asked me if I would meet him at the White Castle near my home. I said okay because it sounded important.

When I got there, he got in my car and asked me to buy him a cup of coffee. I said of course I would. He then told me he wanted to kill himself. His business had gone under, and he owed everyone, especially his brother-in-law. So I said, "Don't kill yourself over money! Get another job and pay them back as you can." He replied, "I'm flat broke." I told him that I could give him a little money to hold him over.

A few days later he called me and said he had found a job. He was so happy that he wanted to take me out to dinner on Saturday. I said okay. But Saturday never came, and I didn't hear from him for three weeks. When I finally met up with him, I knew he was sick. He looked ill. We dated for a few weeks but soon drifted apart again, and actually I was glad.

One night while I was waitressing, the owner of the bar came in and asked if I would like to be a bartender. I was so excited, yet so scared; it was a busy bar. I definitely said yes and would start in three days. The bar owner thought I would draw a crowd. I was what you call curvy, not skinny. I wore pretty clothes (size ten) and jewelry, and my hair was long and wildly moussed.

When I told Allen, he was angry with me for taking the job, probably because there would be too many men. On my first night the bar was packed with people. The manager, who was supposed to finish training me, didn't show up so I was on my own. Allen kept yelling about everything I was doing wrong, but no one else complained. I told him to leave. When Nick and his friends came in, I was already buying free drinks for people. The night was a big success, and the owner was really happy. Nick helped me close the place because the manager was a friend of his and Nick had seen how he did it many times.

I was dating Nick maybe a few times a month, and the dates were always nice. Going out to eat with him was always a pleasure; he made you feel like you could order the whole menu. But the relationship wasn't going anywhere. I was always so unsure where I stood with Nick. Occasionally he did tell me he loved me, and he wasn't the kind of guy who said that easily. He also asked me to move in with him later on, but I couldn't do it.

I was living in the apartment on a side street, where hardly anyone drove by. A friend who lived next door went to the bar Nick frequented and was astonished that almost every day and night Nick drove past my house. He had vanity plates that made his car easy to identify. So when I was talking to Nick, I told him my neighbor saw him go by all the time, and he admitted it. He said even his kids asked him, "Why are you passing back and forth on this block?" This went on for about a year.

Let me tell you about the crank calls. My daughters would tell you that I am probably one of the few people who get excited over crank calls. Let me explain. I knew who was making them, and usually shortly after the crank call came the real call—from Nick. He was notorious for crank calls. I always knew it was him because he would call me from a bar, and once, someone even called his name in the background. He hung up on one occasion. He didn't call on a regular basis so when I got a crank call, I'd get excited; I knew he would be calling.

At that time I was really crazy about him. We were a perfect couple, and he never got angry. We also liked to dance together. In the mid-1980s I fell in love with heavy metal bands like Motley Crue and Guns N' Roses. Thanks to the world of cable, I wore the ripped jeans and band T-shirts that were popular, and I had the shape to do it back then. Still dating Nick, I talked a lot about the music and the bands, but it never took anything away from how I felt about him. He was going bald but it didn't bother me at all.

One weeknight around midnight he came over. As usual he was wearing his baseball cap, but when he came into the kitchen, he took it off and his whole head was shaved. I was shocked. He said maybe his hair would grow back and it would get long. I told him I never cared about that. But when he took the hat off, my daughter, who was in her bedroom watching us, was so shocked she almost fell out of her bunk bed.

I did meet a policeman at another bar, but that relationship didn't last. He was a complete drunk. He even got kicked off the police force because of his drinking.

The few years that I was into the bar scene, I was not an alcoholic nor did I drink a lot. In fact, I didn't even like drinking, but it was a social outlet for me. I did meet a lot of people, and because I was working at the bar close to my house, everyone knew me. I remember my kids asking me why the people I knew didn't have regular names. There was TV Joe, Biker Mike, Cable Tom, Roofer Joe, Irish Mike, and so on. I just kind of laughed and said, "I guess that's what they're known for!"

When you go to bars you do meet a lot of people. Some are your friends and some are backstabbers. I met a man named Gino, who was quite older than I was, but we had a friendship for a brief time. There was absolutely no romance, just laughs and fun—oh, and of course, gossip! When I met him, he did try to date me but realized it wouldn't happen.

One day we made up this little game. We both were known at the bar, so when I wasn't around, he would mention my name to see what people said about me. I would do the same thing with him when I was at the bar. Then we would reveal to each other what everyone said about us. Gosh, it was hysterical! The best time had to be when Gino's best friend, Chuck, sat down next to me and I said, "Have you seen Gino lately?" He replied, "You mean Squeaky? He wears rubber shoes and when he walks, he squeaks. He's so cheap!" Chuck didn't understand why I was laughing so hard. Little did he know it was because I would be telling Gino these very words later on!

I couldn't wait till I saw Gino. A few days went by and we ran into each other. I told him about being called "Squeaky," and he had a fit. Unless you were a woman and he wanted to buy you a drink, Gino was cheap with his friends. I couldn't stop laughing! Then it was his turn. He had talked to an older guy whom I rarely talked to and asked him if he had seen me around lately. The guy replied, "Yeah, she comes around every so often when she has hot pants!" The bad part was we couldn't say anything to any of the people who said things about us because then our game would be over. Oh well, it was so fun that it was worth it! But Gino never lived down being squeaky.

There was a more popular bar a few blocks away, so I went there one night and saw a thin, young-looking guy around 165 pounds with salt-and-pepper hair. Someone said his name was Kevin. I asked him if he was stuck up, but he was busy playing pool so I left. I went there again and this time we talked and he bought me some drinks. We even found out that my sister was married to someone he knew.

Before we left the bar, he asked me for a date and I said yes. There were always long periods of time when I didn't hear from Nick and I was tired of it.

Kevin and I went on the date, and I found out I was eight years older than he was. But we didn't care. I could tell right away he was nuts about me. We went to a lodge, and he even walked me to the bathroom and back. He told me that night, "We're going to get married."

Kevin was always good about anything mechanical. The first time I got cable TV he set it up for me. He could fix just about anything around the house, which was a plus. He was also a good car mechanic. When I was dating him, I took full advantage of these qualities. But my kids and I knew that about every couple of months I got this face. We called it the "gas bill face." Running a two-flat home and paying for the heat and hot water was very expensive. I always had trouble paying the bills. Then it happened: I received a disconnect notice and tried everything in the book to stop it, but it happened. Kevin was there the day the gas company came, and he went to the basement with the guy to shut it off. I was in tears, but Kevin had a smile on his face. When the guy left, he said he had shown Kevin how to turn it back on without the company ever knowing. So Kevin turned it on and then turned it back off before I paid the bill five days later. No one ever knew, not even the company.

He wasn't at all set financially. Kevin repaired cars but didn't make much money. However, I did like him and we seemed to have good chemistry. Before long it was always Kevin and me. I can't say the kids really liked him though, especially Natalie.

During our relationship, Kevin seemed to have a drinking problem, and I told him I was going to break up with him. He started drinking too much, and that was not what I wanted. So he asked me, "If I join AA will you stand by me?" I said okay. He joined and completely quit drinking, and things were going very well. I was shocked though when his mother, Stella, wrote him a letter that said, "Don't let anyone tell you what to do." She was writing about me. I was only trying to help him.

CHAPTER 12

Baby Blessing 3

Months went by, and I had to change my birth control. Wouldn't you know it, the method I got must not have been inserted right, and I became pregnant. I couldn't believe it! I don't think the kids could believe it either, but Chloe was happy. Kevin was happy. His mother said she was happy too. We got married right away. The reception was held at our local VFW, and we invited all our friends and our small amount of family. Everyone had fun except my friend Loni. She acted like she did not want to be there at all. She said she forgot her checkbook and had to leave. Later on down the line I called her mom about a coat I borrowed and she said Loni received an inheritance and didn't need the coat back. She couldn't explain what was wrong with Loni. That was the last I heard from her.

Before Kevin and I got married, he had been in a car accident with a guy who was on drugs. We were separated for a while so maybe Kevin was on drugs too, but he was the passenger so he got a big settlement—well, pretty big when you have nothing. So for our honeymoon we went to the

Sybaris hotel. It was so nice, but I had a sinus headache the entire time. I have to admit it felt better during sex. We went out for a beautiful dinner every night because the hotel had no provisions for food. I only wish the whole marriage could have been like the honeymoon, except for the headache.

It was a difficult pregnancy because I was much older this time around. Kevin wasn't bringing in much money so I also was worried about all kinds of things. His mother wanted to have a shower for me, but my sister Teri wouldn't give her a list of people to invite. But I loved the way it turned out. Kevin's mother gave us a charge card instead and told us to pick whatever we needed for the baby. That was fun! Kevin picked the best of everything!

When I married Kevin, I knew in my heart there were going to be problems, but I did all I could do to suppress them. After all, I was going to be forty years old, and I was pregnant. Kevin was an alcoholic up until a few months before our marriage. He had a mediocre job and still had some of the settlement money from the accident, but I knew that would go pretty fast—and it did.

When we were in the bars, we had a good time and he seemed to really kiss the ground I walked on. This was flattering. But once that piece of paper was signed, things changed. There were stepchildren problems, mother-in-law problems, brother-in-law problems, and worst of all, temper problems. I had a similar problem with him before we married, but I thought it was a one-time thing. I was wrong. So again I'd made a bad decision I was going to have to live with.

Soon after Kevin and I got married, my mother-in-law, Stella, announced that she didn't cook, so she invited us to dinner at a nice restaurant for Thanksgiving. Kevin and I, Chloe, and Kevin's brother joined her for dinner. I was pregnant at the time. The restaurant was delightful and had a museum with antiques. I wasn't interested in antiques, but it was fun to look. Stella fell in love with a clock that cost about $150.

We all ordered the traditional turkey dinner. Natalie had to work so I bought a dinner to take home for her. The food, the atmosphere, and even the conversation were great. I thought this was a lovely holiday until the bill came. Stella said to Kevin, "You pay for your family, and I'll pay for your brother." I couldn't believe it. She invited us because she didn't want to cook and then made us pay our own bill. Kevin tried not to let it bother him, but he was hurt and embarrassed. I couldn't count how many dinners I had cooked for his family, and I enjoyed cooking them too. It certainly wasn't about the money. Who knows why she did this? And now I can say, "Who cares?" I couldn't have guessed that Christmas would be even worse!

I thought the first Christmas Kevin and I spent together would be wonderful. We decorated the house, and it looked beautiful. We were invited to his aunt's house, and everyone knew that Kevin, Chloe, Natalie, and I were going to be there. My kids weren't that old, so I asked Kevin's mother if I should bring presents for them to open and she said no. We had to pay to go, which I had never heard of before. But Kevin's mother described it so well: "shrimp, Italian beef, ham, salads, etc." So we didn't mind pitching in to go to his aunt's house. Well, when we got there, the shrimp were already gone, the beef was cold, and the salads were all torn apart. There were generic chips and soda, but I could deal with that. When we walked in, I gave Kevin's aunt a nice tin of cookies and Kevin had about twenty envelopes with thirty dollars in each of them as gifts.

After dinner the main event of the night began: the exchanging of gifts. The names were being called right and left. Kevin and his mother were getting gifts, but my kids were getting nothing. I was disgusted and humiliated. Nice welcome to the family! My kids and I just sat there, the only ones in the whole place without gifts. I had ruined my kids' Christmas Eve. I felt like there was no consideration on the part of Kevin's relatives for his family, so I told Kevin not to pass out those envelopes. He didn't and I was glad. It was one of the worst Christmas Eves we ever had, and Kevin said he was ashamed of his family.

The next morning, after the kids opened their presents and went to their dad's house, I went to tell Teri what happened. She opened the door, and when I started to tell her about Christmas Eve, she slammed the door in my face. Believe it or not, I wasn't surprised she took the family's side over mine.

Toward the end of my pregnancy, Kevin was on the phone with his mother a lot and mentioned having his brother as the baby's godfather. I squirmed inside but didn't say anything. I didn't want him as godfather. Later that night Kevin asked me to take a ride with him to get gas and I did. He told me he wanted his brother to be the godfather. I said that I didn't, and he slapped me in the face. I told him to get out of my house. And guess what? He went straight to his mother's house. I was eight months pregnant and upset about this. Well, he came back and we didn't discuss godparents, but things were different.

Eventually I believe being sober was really affecting Kevin. He was becoming moody, and if we had an argument, he would give me the silent treatment for days. He had a younger brother, Tommy, who never wanted for anything in his life because Kevin's mother adored him and gave him whatever he desired. She rented the upstairs apartment in my building for him. Kevin and his brother had a sister who died, and Tommy was selling her belongings for money. Kevin had a fit. All Tommy was doing was drinking at the bars every day. His mom even bought him a new car and within two weeks he totaled it.

The night I went into labor, Kevin told the hospital he wanted the bill in his name not mine. Even though I had health insurance, he said, "I want to be responsible for it." When Kevin left the room, the attendant said, "Should I put it on the insurance?" and I said yes.

Well, I had an adorable seven-pound, seven-ounce girl whom I named Lauren. She looked like a miniature punk rocker because she had lots of spiked hair. Chloe and Natalie fell in love with her immediately too. I don't know what I would have done without them.

Kevin was going to be gone for three days, helping his mother move back from another state. Everything was pretty good at this time, so I decided to dye my hair blond and surprise him. Now I had thick, dark brown hair and dark brown eyebrows, so this would be a drastic change. I went to a salon that I thought would do a great job, but what a shock I had. The stylist left the bleach on too long and my hair was white when it was done. She also had put some dye on my eyebrows, but they looked like a leopard. It was terrible; I kept thinking of David Bowie.

I went to my daughter Natalie's house and she was shocked. We went to pick up Lauren at my sister's house and she was afraid of me. I should have taken a picture and sued the beautician. Natalie bought dye and we tried to re-dye it dark brown, but it turned out to be a brown/green color. It was horrible. I told the stylist I had pictures and would sue if I didn't get a refund, and I did get my money back. But it took about a year to get my hair back to normal. I should have sued, another bad decision I had to live with!

When Lauren was a baby I told Kevin to get another side job, but he ignored me. So I got a job and went right to work, thanks to my daughters keeping an eye on Lauren. But then my daughters started calling me at work to tell me that Kevin wasn't going to work. Although I was kind of afraid of him, one night when the older girls were out of the house, I said to him, "What the hell's going on? I get a job and now you're taking off! What's this crap?" He picked up the DVD player and threw it at me, almost hitting the baby. He went to punch me but the baby was screaming, so he just walked out. I was so relieved that he left.

When Natalie came home, I told her what had happened and we talked about going to the police because the DVD player could have killed the baby. I couldn't have this violence around my children. We filed a report, but I had to go back to the police station the next day to get an order of protection. When Kevin came back to the house around eleven o'clock, he was drunk. I wanted him out so I told him to leave. I also said that I had gone to the police and they would be serving him the papers the next day at work. So he left. I was both relieved and sad but safe!

This time Kevin was gone for a long time, and his mother, who never wanted anything to do with him, bought him a bed. According to him, he had to pay her money to live there. So you can figure where that left me.

Kevin and I had been separated for a couple of months when I decided to get Lauren baptized. After not seeing him for a while, I agreed to meet Kevin a few weeks after the baptism, which he knew nothing about. He was back to drinking, and I wanted no part of that, but I gave in to talk. He picked me up at the house and we drove to a park. A few minutes into the conversation something didn't feel right. Kevin was telling me he wanted to come back to Lauren and me and help us. It sounded good so I decided to tell him about the baptism. I actually think something snapped in his brain because he went nuts, and I then smelled the alcohol on his breath. What was I going to do? He was like a wild man. I thought he was going to kill me. We were right by a lagoon, so I was scared. Kevin didn't like my choice of godparents, Mickey and her boyfriend, although they were good to Lauren. I told him we could say they were temporary until he and I agreed on permanent godparents. Then I saw a huge bag of laundry in the backseat, so I said, "Why don't I do your laundry? We'll take it to the house, and when I explain to the kids that you're coming back in a couple of days, all your clothes will be there." That worked. When we got back to my house, I said, "Let me go in first to see if the kids are here, and if they aren't, you can bring the laundry in." I was shaking all over because I had never seen him so mad; I knew he was going to kill me.

When I got in the house, I locked the outside door and the inside door, and then I opened the window and screamed that we were not getting back together and that I was going to stay far away from him. He left, but I found it hard to sleep that night. I must confess I said something else too that I won't repeat, but it felt great!

During this time, I went to the gas station, the one where Kevin slapped me, and ran into Nick. He said my sister had told him I got married, and he hated her for that. I told him the marriage was over as fast as it happened. We went out a few times, but I was too focused on the baby and working. I spent a lot of time with my daughters so I didn't want to go to the bars as much.

I had to deal with a lot of health problems, but I did go with my daughter Natalie to a Bon Jovi concert. We ran into Kevin's friends, which upset me because I knew they'd tell him and he'd be mad. Don't ask me why, but I just knew he would be mad. The next day was Sunday and I was baking chicken and my friend Mickey was over. The doorbell rang and I answered it. It was Kevin with diapers and milk. Lauren had turned a year old, but Kevin didn't even look at her. He asked me if I wanted to take a ride to the lake, but I declined. He said, "Why?" I said, "I don't care to go." I had Lauren in my arms, and all of a sudden he started to beat me excessively in the face and head. I felt part of my lip missing. Mickey and the kids called the police and tried to help, but they were scared too. When the tenants upstairs came home, they thought there had been a massacre in the hallway. Lauren never got a scratch on her since I held her close to my chest.

When I got to the hospital, a plastic surgeon was called in because a quarter of my top lip was gone. When the police came and then saw all the police reports, they called in the state's attorney.

When I look back on the few months we were together, there were a lot of red flags. He had a hot temper and a part of me was afraid of him. So I wasn't entirely shocked by the outcome.

At the time I was beat up, I had a pretty good job as a data entry clerk. The pay was good. But I had to tell them what had happened to me and that my ex-husband was now in prison. Their faces told it all. I looked horrible with all the cuts and bruises on my face. Everywhere I went people would stare at me. My boss told me that having me come back would be unsafe because Kevin could get out of prison, so I lost my job. Another strike against me.

Kevin was charged with aggravated stalking because there were tons of police reports on him bothering me and threatening me on the phone. He got seven years and three months, and that was the end of him for a few years. He would be getting out for good behavior later on.

After Kevin was sentenced and the case was closed, someone came to the door. I guess when Kevin beat me up so severely there was someone waiting for him in the car—a guy named Rich. I knew him from just seeing him around. He claimed he didn't know at first what Kevin was planning to do, but if I would have gone to the lake that day, he would have gotten rid of me. He said he wanted to apologize and see if I needed him to testify. I said no but thank you. Thank God I didn't go with Kevin that day.

While he was in prison, Kevin's mom contacted me and wanted to see Lauren that Christmas. She took pictures of Lauren and me and mailed them to Kevin. He wrote me a letter thanking me for the pictures. I had asked her not to send Kevin pictures, so I didn't see much of her after that.

Lauren's godparents were moving to the suburbs, so I decided to sell my place and move too. The apartment building sold pretty quickly. I had taken out a second mortgage, but I still had quite a bit of money left. I got a job in fine retail, but the pay was awful and all I did was worry about money. The rents were very high, and I had to take most of the rent out of the bank. Before I knew it, my bank account was almost empty. Mickey and her boyfriend had two incomes; I had one and made very little money. I ended up moving back to the neighborhood a year later; I was broke so I got a job waitressing. Only Lauren and Chloe were living with me; Natalie had moved in with her father for more freedom. I had different guys work on the car or fix things for me, but then they would solicit me for sex. So that wasn't working out at all.

Lauren envied Chloe and Natalie because they went to Catholic school, but it was impossible to send her on my own. I had no help at all. She did make her communion and much later her confirmation. I was very proud of her for doing this and making her religion a priority. As far as Lauren wanting for things, I really don't think she did without anything. There were a few good years when her paternal grandmother helped a lot with material things, and that was appreciated.

Unfortunately, Lauren's grandmother moved out of state suddenly to be with her son. Lauren was devastated because as she got older she liked to visit her grandma, although Lauren sat in her home for five to six hours and wasn't even offered a glass of water. I doubt she was happy to see Lauren. To be honest, she told Lauren not to come, but Lauren went there anyway. She hasn't been back since, but she really loves her grandmother. My parents died years ago so she never had any grandparents on my side.

Kevin's father, Lauren's grandfather, didn't have a lot to do with her at all. But once, I had a big Christmas dinner and invited Kevin's parents to it, and they both showed up. I went all out for the dinner. I had food, drinks, beautiful decorations, and presents. That's when Lauren really got to know him; he played with her and gave her beautiful gifts. They seemed to bond. Kevin's father and his wife spent much of their time in another state with Kevin's brother, who lived with them. The most terrible thing happened to his father: he died at the hands of his own son.

Apparently Kevin's brother, Tommy, beat up their father and kicked him in the head. An ambulance took him to the hospital for a concussion, and the doctor wanted him to spend the night—he was in his seventies—but he wouldn't do it. He died a few hours later at home. The newspaper headline read "Son Kills Father." Kevin was devastated. He had been drinking and we were splitting up, so after this he got worse. I know he was on drugs so I told him to go. I had never dealt with a drug addict and wasn't going to start. I didn't see him after that for a few years. My mother-in-law hired a high-priced attorney for Tommy who found a supposed loophole to get him out of the charges. But to everyone involved it was obvious why a man in good health would die after being severely hit and kicked in the head. Money bought this kind of justice.

The worst job I ever had was working at the ballpark for a major league team. Nothing against them, but it was horrible. It could have been the people I worked with. I was working the concession stand, and my daughter Natalie was an usher. Throughout the day she would visit me with cold rags and wipe my face. I would work six hours straight, and by then I would need to use the restroom. I was told, "No, you can't close the line!" Of course, they closed the line when they had to use the restroom!

The first day I was there, money went missing and of course they accused me. I was new and that was convenient. I never took a dime or a thing to eat. All I cared about was getting my work done and going home. After about three weeks, I quit. I do believe it was the people I worked with. Also I had family that worked there, including my mom, and I understand they were angry that I quit. All I have to say to them is too bad, be mad! No one should work under those conditions.

I dated a bartender for a while, and he eventually asked me to move in with him. Then he turned goofy. He became mean and wanted a lot of money and threatened to turn me in to DCFS (Department of Children and Family Services) if I left his house. I was there three weeks. He even kept my bed and many other items of mine. Then he repeated something I had said and couldn't wait to get me in all kinds of trouble. Real nice guy.

I was talking to my sister on and off around this time, and Teri called and told me Kevin wanted to help me. I had gotten a new apartment, my car wasn't running, and I was flat broke so I said okay. Kevin fixed the car and gave me money. Apparently he had served his time, and we eventually got back together. We got another apartment, but he broke his toe and could not work. Then, to top it off,

Kevin's brother, Tommy, beat up his dad so bad that he *died* from his injuries. Kevin wanted to kill his brother and was drunk from morning till night. After the funeral he kept demanding all the money in the house. I didn't trust him so I told him to get out and lied that I had gotten another order of protection. He left with $5,000, his income tax refund and insurance settlement for his toe. It only lasted a couple of months. We never were together as a couple again.

Around the time Kevin and I split up, I was going through a difficult time. My life had been turned upside down. I had no money, was raising a baby alone, and had no one to turn to. So I went to talk to a priest at my church. He could see how overwhelmed I was, and we even talked about my first marriage to Carl that had taken place in that church. He was horrified by my stories and advised me to get an annulment from Carl and to divorce Kevin and do it immediately. He gave me a lot of paperwork to do and told me to bring it back when I was done. The paperwork involved just about our entire life together, at least Carl's and mine. It must have taken three days, and when I brought the papers back, the priest asked if I'd, had an attorney type them. I said, "No, I did it myself." I had at least 150 pages of significant life events that I needed to submit.

My next step was to see a type of mediator at another church, and she was the kindest nun. She had already read my papers and said, "I'm sure you'll be granted an annulment. But this is just the first step." She told me there could or could not be a charge for the annulment. She also asked me to pray for her, which I did daily, because she had breast cancer.

I started receiving mail from the tribunal office downtown. I had to see a psychiatrist and a counselor. After that I was told I would receive a letter with the decision. On my own, I wrote a letter to Pope John Paul asking him to pray that I would get the annulment. I also wrote to him, asking if I could write a book and devote it to him. He gave me his blessing.

There was silence for quite a while. Every day I would check the mailbox, but nothing came. Eventually I did receive two letters from the pope, and I was very happy! It had to be about eight months later that the letter came, and I was granted the annulment. I was so excited! I felt like a new person. I wasn't charged for the annulment either. Double plus!

That night I sat at the kitchen table and had a drink and felt God all around me. It was beautiful!

CHAPTER 13

Hit Squad for Idle Gossip

Not all my acquaintances were men. I did have female friends. One in particular was Jill. She was by no means a shy person but very outspoken. She was a little older than me and seemed to always know what was going on in the neighborhood. She had a grown son she seemed to cater to and often talked about her family's affiliation with the mafia. Not surprising in my neighborhood! Whenever I saw Jill, it was at her house to pick up products I bought from the cosmetics line she worked for or to help her make her cosmetic deliveries. We went to the bar together a few times, but she mainly liked to play poker. I liked to mingle. She had never been to my house, but I had gone to see her once when I was troubled and left the same way. I went to the store for her a few times but never minded because I liked her and considered her a good friend.

Jill had a rich uncle, supposedly connected to the mafia, who lived around the corner from her. One weekend she asked me to go to her uncle's house with her, and I did, with Lauren in tow. The house was practically a mansion, but sadly the uncle was dying. For many reasons I was glad we left. The uncle died a few months later. I didn't attend the funeral since I didn't really know him and Jill had tons of people who came for her. I stopped hearing too much from Jill, but then I ran into her and found out she was spending a lot of time with her aunt, her uncle's widow. She told me the aunt was severely depressed and was trying to stop gambling. She even went to a priest. Jill said that she, her aunt, and her friend rode in a limousine every weekend to the casino. It didn't make sense to me, but I kept my thoughts to myself. Sometime after that I went in the local VFW and the bartender told me Jill's aunt had died. I made a smart remark about her aunt and uncle, and you can be sure it got right back to Jill. I'll never know why I made the remark to backstabbing bar people. But I did and I paid for it!

Before I knew it, I had a hit squad on me. That was confirmed when Jill called me and said, "Be careful and watch Lauren! I don't know what to tell you, but things are crazy!" That's what she said to me.

They were doing everything you could think of, such as ransacking my apartment, stealing from me, and stalking me. A certain bar owner with vanity plates (Nick) kept driving past my house over and over. My landlord said the bar owner told him to evict me, but he couldn't because I didn't owe any rent. No one would believe me except my doctor because he knew the neighborhood well. I didn't think they wanted to kill me but maybe drive me crazy. I didn't call the police because I didn't trust them and knew they wouldn't believe me! At the time I thought they might kill me. There was a monastery in the neighborhood and the monks believed me and prayed for me. I went to church one day and was in deep prayer when all of a sudden I saw an apparition: Mary nursing baby Jesus. I was in awe and just kept staring; the feeling was wonderful. I'd never seen things that weren't there. I only told those at the monastery about the apparition, and they believed me completely. I've never forgotten this time in my life; it has helped me get through terrible ordeals.

Nobody was coming around, and my kids thought I was crazy. Then the phone rang; it was Nick at two o'clock in the afternoon. I was surprised because he had to know what was going on. He asked if he could come over because he got me something. I said okay. He came by and brought all kinds of gifts for me, including candles. I was so surprised. I should have known something was wrong while I was talking to him. He seemed aggravated when he answered me. But he asked to see me that Saturday, and I said yes.

On Saturday night I lit the candles all over the house, and Nick arrived around nine o'clock. Lauren was in bed. He rang the bell and I let him in. As he was taking off his jacket, he said, "I was just at the club with a bunch of guys and guess who was there?" He then told me he was at the club with Jill's deceased uncle. I was furious and told him to put his jacket on and get the hell out. I said, "You've thrown away all these years we've known each other to play with my mind like everyone else. You're no longer anything to me." He left immediately.

It must have been around two o'clock the next morning when my phone rang. It was Nick, and I could hardly understand him. He sounded like he was crying or upset. He said, "You don't understand. They made me do it; they wouldn't leave me alone." I said, "I'm sorry but I don't trust you anymore. Anyone who plays with my mind isn't trustworthy." I never saw him again.

The next day I decided to get a holy card for support. When I went to the religious store, Nick's friends pulled up in a car. They must have followed me. They told me to get Nick a holy card too! They must have known why I was there or figured it out. I never knew why these people bothered Nick if they did. I had nothing to tell Nick. Only God knows why I said and did the things I did. Never would I confide in Nick, so he knew nothing about my dealings with Jill.

What's funny is when I first dated Nick, he borrowed money from the wrong people for a grocery store he wanted to buy. At first the store was doing well, but as time went on it started falling apart. A backstabbing friend of his told me that customers just got tired of "It's a little over, okay?" His friend explained that Nick would always try to sneak more meat on the scale, but I never believed that. All his friends talked behind his back and used to ask me why I was with him. When Nick couldn't make the payments he owed these bad people, they cut the wires to his coolers, which held the meat and dairy products. I even got a call that there was a hit on him and to be careful. Nick said everything was okay, but one night we went to his apartment and had to cut through the store to get to it. The odor from the rotting meat was pure hell! I never made a big deal about it but sure didn't go back. These were the people for whom he was going to hurt me.

About a year later Nick took me out on a boat where he told me he was in love with me, and it wasn't for sex.

CHAPTER 14

God Blesses Me

In the midst of all the problems in my life, I had a true blessing happen. I went to the grocery store and was in line to pay for my groceries when an elderly woman told the cashier she had just seen the pope. The cashier seemed excited and so was I. The cashier asked if she could touch her, and the lady said yes. I, in turn, asked if I could touch her, and she said yes. I was elated. After I paid for my groceries, I walked outside to get in my car and heard a Spanish man screaming, "My baby's dead; it's not breathing!" I held the baby close to my heart and began rocking her. The baby began coughing and breathing and got really hot. We took the baby into the pharmacy and wiped her with cool wipes, but the pharmacy called the paramedics and they took over. The father thanked me because the baby had not been breathing. It's a beautiful story that I'll never forget! I saved three other lives in different ways but nothing so miraculous as this one.

I've stayed out in the suburbs and don't look back at anything that happened in that old house or that old neighborhood. I rent an apartment with Lauren, who's still at home. Once in a while I talk to Kevin, but he's in and out of rehab. Lauren can't stand him. He once came to our apartment unannounced, and Lauren and her boyfriend were in her bedroom. He looked through the window and went after her and struck her. He was a maniac. She won't forgive him, but he doesn't remember hitting her. Kevin's mother disowned him, but she has kept in contact with the son who ended his father's life.

Now that I've been able to clear myself through prayer of all the people who hurt me both physically and mentally, I have a much better life, and I'm such an obedient person. I don't push my religion on people, but I pray for people and I'm amazed at the results. Prayers certainly have changed my life. Don't get me wrong; I'm by no means a saint. I've done terrible things in my life, but I know by the life I lead now I have been forgiven.

In 2012 my health was starting to change. One day I had an unbelievable headache. Now, I suffered from headaches a lot but nothing like this. The next day I went out and the sun was shining, and the vision in my right eye was bad. I went to the eye doctor, who put me right in the hospital. I had suffered a ministroke in that eye and lost a third of my vision.

The following year I was in bad pain and went back and forth for MRIs of my head and spine. The tests showed a large tumor on my adrenal gland. The doctor thought it was cancer but couldn't do a biopsy because of the tumor's location. So I had surgery, which left me very ill. I was losing six to eight pounds a week and was down to 110 pounds. My doctor thought I was dying. People stared at me because I looked anorexic. That's why I continued to pray, and all of a sudden I was fine again.

That same year, however, I got more bad news; I had cancer of the vulva. The operation wasn't bad and the surgeon got it all, but I had a headache for days after the procedure. Following that surgery, I kept experiencing shortness of breath but thought it was stress. One night I finally went to the emergency room and was told I needed a pacemaker. I was admitted right away. Eight hours went by and I lay there the whole time. I kept calling the nurse but the staff was mean, so I signed out AMA (against medical advice). I was referred to a cardiologist and told him I needed a pacemaker, so he admitted me right away. After the surgery, I felt a lot better.

At the end of 2013 I was suffering from a toothache and needed a bridge on my bottom teeth. I hadn't been to the dentist in a while and already had dentures on top. I found a nice family dental practice and went for a consultation. I had a woman dentist who seemed kind and very professional. She gave me a thorough checkup with X-rays and told me the problem was the front right tooth on the bottom. There were two teeth in this spot though, and I told her I felt pain in the other tooth too. She said, "No, you have a cavity with an infected nerve, and it needs to come out immediately." She claimed it was severely rotted. I was surprised because the outside of the tooth showed no decay at all.

Well, she was the professional so I made a plan to fix my teeth. The plan would be close to $2,000. She said I needed to go to an oral surgeon or another dentist to have the tooth pulled because she didn't extract teeth. She gave me papers to show the doctor who would pull the tooth.

I called some oral surgeons but they were too expensive, and then I found a dentist. He looked at the tooth and said there was nothing wrong with it. The first thing that went through my mind was that I had just agreed to $2,000 in credit that had to be paid back to a bank. I hope I had made the right decision. The dentist asked me if he could X-ray it for no charge. That's how sure he was that the tooth was fine. He found no decay. So I called the new dentist who said, "I don't know what kind of X-ray machine he has, but the tooth is full of infection and decay."

So, the dentist who was going to extract the tooth had me sign a statement that said he wasn't responsible for the tooth being in good health. Sure enough, the pulled tooth was snow white and had no decay at all. The dentist also informed me that I could never have a bridge without that pulled tooth. (Actually, he told me that in the early stage of this fiasco.)

I was upset and felt cheated. I called the family practice and said the tooth was not decayed at all and I was not getting my teeth done there or paying them a dime. They kept calling me for weeks. The CEO of the practice said he'd do my teeth, but I declined because they were still saying the tooth was bad. I finally said, "I have the tooth and a letter from the dentist. What more proof do I need? I'm ready to sue you." Then I got a letter and a call from the bank. It picked up the $2,000 I owed for the dental plan I agreed to. I stayed with the dentist who did the extraction.

Shockingly enough, after that I got news, my daughter Natalie called me and said she and her husband, Dan, were treating me to a cruise to the Bahamas. I was so excited and had just gotten a credit card, so I was set. It was the most wonderful trip in the world—the beautiful islands, the vibrant blue ocean, the delectable food, and richness all around us. I felt like I didn't have a care in the world. My daughter's mother-in-law came too. Things were a little hard for her because she has ALS, so I tried to help her when I could. But that's definitely a goal for me now: to go on another cruise.

When the cruise was over, everything went back to normal until I got a letter in the mail. My mammogram showed something suspicious so I had to go in for another test. I had breast cancer. But, thank God, it was stage one. I only needed radiation, but because my pacemaker was so close to the cancer, it was difficult to get in there during surgery. It turned out I had to walk around with eight wires in my breast during the entire treatment and they were very painful. But the doctor got all the cancer and there was no cancer in the lymph nodes.

They say the more you suffer, the closer you get to God. I do believe that. I sure have had my share of suffering throughout my life. Now I feel my life has become calmer and more peaceful, and I'm so thankful.

I have a rewarding job working for and helping the elderly. I never knew how helpless some of us get as we age, and I never thought I would be in a position to help anyone. A lot of the elderly are lonely and just need companionship. They really appreciate what I do, and that makes me happy.

Of course, I have my bad habits—Diet Pepsi and smoking, but not as much. I don't drink alcohol because it interferes with my medications, and I stopped going out to bars years ago. But I certainly don't condemn people who drink or go to bars. In fact, most people would find my life boring. But it's a good change for me compared to the days when I was a human punching bag. No one is yelling at me or calling me filthy names or putting me down. All that mental abuse took years to get out of my head. I walked around thinking I'd never be anything because that was pounded into my head like a form of brainwashing. It took a long time to clear my mind. When I finally got out of these situations, I was a different person. I learned to make more intelligent decisions with no regrets.

I can't say there were never any good times in these violent relationships, but the violence, disrespect, and humiliation outweighed them. I could have easily died in those terrible instances, and my children suffered. I'm glad all our suffering is over and I have healed. I didn't have much therapy for my domestic violence issues; my healing came from God.

Well, I'm up in age now so I don't think about romance like I used to. I don't necessarily think I'll never date again, but it's not a priority. If it crosses my path again someday, fine. If not, it's not meant to be. I'm not at all anti-men. It's just not at the top of my list right now.

I will tell you one thing: you have to learn to stand on your own two feet. But we all need support, and I've had a few angels in my life who have helped me: my late landlord and his wife, the St. Vincent De Paul Society, and my daughters. Without these people I wouldn't have lived decently. Yes, these people were angels on earth to me.

I seriously hope my book helps someone in a bad place, maybe a victim of domestic violence. Know that there's a way out. It won't happen overnight, but you can make a plan and stick to it. A supportive family helps too because in my case, it was a friend and a prayer.

I wanted to write this book because I recognized, even as a child, that I have led a highly unusual life. For so many years I lived in a shell, letting people take advantage of me, in other words walk all over me. I was always a kind person. I gave them so much, not only material things but also any help they needed. To this very day I'm the same, but I've learned who is trustworthy.

I don't have to care about all the people who hurt me anymore. I can stand up for myself, thanks to God. And now the decisions I make don't cause conflicting situations. To live with peace in my heart and mind is a wonderful thing, especially when I was almost in a state of insanity at various points in my life. I had to give up these situations of abuse, power, jealousy, mind games, and lies and only be with the people who didn't hurt me and who cared about me.

So when I decided to write the book, I got nothing but support from my daughters. And writing the book let me breathe again.

Now when I hear about or see anything that concerns domestic abuse, I get angry. I forget where I was years ago and how long I put up with it, and I can't for one minute understand why people stay in these relationships. In my heart I know all the reasons why, and it's mainly fear. In my case there was no support, no place or person to turn to. Now there's a lot more of this. Finances are another big reason why people stay. I remember going to a domestic violence center in the eighties with my daughter Lauren. We had no money and were there for hours. I asked if they had a cookie for my daughter since we didn't plan on being there that long. They said no, and I was surprised. They were supposed to call me back about some funding but never did. So I took a ride to the center and found out the state had stopped its funds because of fraud.

Inner strength is what I needed. I found it by praying. Because I had a medical problem from so much trauma to my head, I see a psychiatrist to this day. When I finally got my divorce from Kevin, it was hard, but I think everyone reaches his or her boiling point, and I had reached mine.

Music always has helped me through tough times. I loved music growing up. The first record I bought was "Big Girls Don't Cry," by the Four Seasons. (Yes, I said "record.") But I liked all kinds of music. I started to listen to rock music by performers like Peter Frampton, ELO, and of course, the Beatles. As I got older, I remember Saturday night used to be "Dusty's night" on the black radio station. This was all R and B music. I was married to Carl at the time, but my friend Mickey would come over and we would drink a little and then just relax and enjoy. I'm sure it's the same for everyone: certain songs make you think of that certain someone. There was a song way back that was playing the first time I danced with Carl called "You've Made Me So Very Happy" by Blood, Sweat & Tears. In spite of all the hell in our marriage, I still feel the same way now as I did back then.

Any Phil Collins or Lionel Richie song always reminds me of Nick. He also looked like Phil Collins. "Penny Lover" by Lionel was our song. In the late eighties, my love was hard rock music. I usually thought of Kevin with those songs. I think if it wasn't for music in my life, a lot of my memories would fade away, but the music keeps them alive!

If you are in a domestic violence situation, a close, caring family is such a plus. I lacked that in my situation. My family, including my mother and sisters, knew that Carl beat me, but they all defended him. I can laugh at that now even though at the time it was unbelievable to me. My sisters adored this man and let me know I was the bad person. They said I deserved what I got. The violence was so overwhelming I couldn't sleep or barely eat.

Carl's words were so right when it came to my sisters: "Misery loves company." They loved when my life was miserable. Sadly, enough, that's how it was because of the abuse. When I was on my own and trying to make it and things started going good, they were angry with me. Why? Because their lives were miserable. So when mine was worse, they felt better.

Leaving Carl, moving out on my own, and working was a huge accomplishment, but Keri was angry because she was jealous. She would have loved to leave her husband for cheating on her, but she couldn't. Unfortunately she then got ill, but the terrible way she treated me was so plain to see.

And after my fire, when Teri left me that couple of dollars, she didn't even ask where me and the kids would stay that night. She didn't realize I had homeowner's insurance, and I didn't tell her. So when the kids and I were getting new clothes and having the house remodeled after the fire, she was mad. She wanted me to be homeless and miserable. She stayed angry with me for about two years.

As far as traveling in my life, I did travel with Carl. We went to Florida, Las Vegas, Wisconsin, and California. We stopped in Tennessee and Georgia but didn't stay. It was pretty enjoyable except for the robbery I mentioned earlier in Fort Lauderdale and the abuse. Kevin and I only went to Indiana, where his family lived, and we took my kids. We did stay at the Sybaris after we got married for three nights since Kevin didn't like to fly. That was pretty romantic at the time.

As I mentioned earlier, my daughter Natalie and her husband took me on a cruise to the Bahamas, and it was magnificent. I felt the closest I've ever been to God. The ship was elaborate and had everything you could think of. Everyone was so friendly, especially the help. I can hardly describe the food, which you could enjoy twenty-four hours a day. This trip was a dream come true, and my next trip will be another cruise. I hope it happens soon.

I decided to do some updates on people in my life who were mentioned in my story. I thought you, the reader, might be curious about how their lives turned out and where they are in my life today.

My oldest brother, Tom, and I barely spoke. My older kids, Chloe and Natalie, knew they had an uncle, and Lauren met him maybe once or twice but never got to know him. In the last few years, he became ill and I was told he wanted to speak to me. I was going into the hospital for my pacemaker surgery and not working at the time, but my sister Teri said, "Please call him," and so I did. Although I tried to talk to him, he was very ill and his wife screened his calls. I never spoke to him again, and he passed away.

After Tom died, his wife was secretive about a lot of stuff, such as where the wake and the funeral would be.

The funeral arrangements weren't in the newspapers as far as I knew. Teri called and asked me to go with her to the wake. She knew I was broke but offered to pay. She had all the information so I said okay, although I hated relying on her for anything. On the day of the wake, we took a cab downtown to the train station. She kept leaving me and making phone calls. This went on for about forty-five minutes. All of a sudden, she told me she didn't know the way and we were going back home. What could I do? So when we got to her house, I went home.

The next day Tom's wife and daughter called and told me that Teri said we didn't come because she lost me and I went to a bar and got drunk. They didn't believe Teri. They called her every filthy name you could think of. They said they would call me and see how I was after my pacemaker surgery. I never heard from them again, but I wasn't surprised.

When I told Teri what they told me, she said they lied. I believed them, not Teri. I wasn't getting along with my kids at the time, so Teri said, "No matter what, I'll be at your pacemaker surgery." She came nowhere near the hospital that day, and again I wasn't surprised.

Teri lied to me about everything and hurt me repeatedly. When her son got cancer, she deliberately cut me out of their lives. Thank God everything turned out well for him. My daughters have told me he is cancer free. Teri told everyone that I didn't do anything to help them. I did send my nephew a prayer card that meant a lot to me. So I tried to do *something* for him.

Then, in a strange turn of events, I got breast cancer and didn't even receive a get-well card. There was no love lost between us, and I'm better off without her in my life.

You would think Keri, being the older sister, would be a role model for me, but she wasn't at all. When I was young, I loved to go to her house and clean it and babysit my nieces. When Keri's kids was born, I had the house cleaned perfectly for each baby's homecoming. She wasn't into cleaning. Whenever Keri went anywhere, I'd run over there to babysit and never got paid. I did the same thing for my brother Tom.

The way I was treated down the line was pathetic. Keri got very ill not long after my mom died. She needed heart surgery, and in the midst of everything, she told me her husband was cheating on her. She caught him. She also was upset about her kids being wild and staying out all hours of the night. She was depressed about everything.

She knew Carl and I were getting an annulment, and when I came to visit her, she got upset because my hair looked nice and I was doing well. I was happy this bothered her so much. She bragged that Carl visited her and made her proud. I said, "Good!" I went to touch her hand and she said, "Don't, that hurts!" That was the last time I saw her. She died a few days later, but first she called to tell me she was going to die, that God had told her this. Everyone at the wake and funeral adored Carl and hated me, but I didn't care.

Keri's husband sued the hospital for her death and got a large settlement. He married the woman with whom he had cheated. He didn't have too much luck because the woman became crippled and, I think, lost her legs. So karma does happen. As for my nieces, I don't know them well.

The last time I heard from my brother Arthur, he requested me as a friend on Facebook. So, being curious, I accepted. I still haven't talked to him in twenty-three years. He chose Carl as a friend over me as his sister. When he saw on Facebook that I had cancer, he still didn't talk to me. I dumped him as a Facebook friend.

Nick, my ex-boyfriend, meant so much to me for so long, but after that incident when he played with my mind and said a man who had died was with him, we never came face-to-face with each other again. I did hear many things about his failing health. The last I heard his legs were going to be amputated because of bad circulation from heart disease and diabetes. One night before Teri and I stopped talking, she called me and told me Nick had died in a car accident. He supposedly went off an expressway.

I try to not think about him with bitterness because he said they made him do it. He said he was being threatened. He also gave me something very intimate to prove he wasn't lying. I didn't attend his wake or funeral. I didn't want to feel uncomfortable. I never really knew his family; I did my mourning with God. Besides, maybe some of the mean people he told me about would have been there. He did tell me a lot, even who they were.

My children, who I feel in most ways I raised myself, are doing very well. They're all adults now and productive members of society. They've all had some college and have earned various degrees. One of them is still working on her degree. Sure, there have been ups and downs in our lives, but now everything is on the up. That's how you have to take life sometimes. Despite the downs, you can't give up.

I haven't dated anyone in years. That's okay with me at this point. I've tried to keep in touch with my family, but it's in vain and I don't care at all anymore. I'm lucky to have six grandchildren who, I have to say, I don't get to see often enough. I'm sure someday that will improve. All in all, I'm very blessed and lucky with a wonderful family.